The Spirit Of Counsel

The Spirit Of Counsel

Spiritual Perspectives in the Counselling Process

Martin Israel

MOWBRAY
LONDON & OXFORD

The scripture quotations in this book are from the New English Bible.

Copyright © 1983 by Martin Israel

First published 1983 by Hodder & Stoughton Limited.
This paperback edition published 1987 by
A.R. Mowbray & Co. Ltd.,
Saint Thomas House, Becket Street,
Oxford, OX1 1SJ

Printed in Great Britain by Richard Clay Ltd, Suffolk.

British Library Cataloguing in Publication Data

Israel, Martin
    The spirit of counsel.
    1. Pastoral counselling
    I. Title
    253.5   BV4012.2

ISBN 0 264 67138 4

Contents

Then a shoot shall grow from the stock of
   Jesse,
     and a branch shall spring from his roots.
The spirit of the Lord shall rest upon him,
     a spirit of wisdom and understanding,
     a spirit of counsel and power,
     a spirit of knowledge and the fear of the
       Lord.

Isaiah 11:1–2

For how can any man learn what is God's plan?
How can he apprehend what the Lord's will is?
The reasoning of men is feeble, and our plans
are fallible; because a perishable body weighs
down the soul, and its frame of clay burdens
the mind so full of thoughts. With difficulty we
guess even at things on earth, and laboriously
find out what lies before our feet; and who has
ever traced out what is in heaven? Who ever
learnt to know thy purposes, unless thou hadst
given him wisdom and sent thy holy spirit
down from heaven on high?

Wisdom of Solomon 9:13–17

Foreword

Counselling assumes an increasing importance in the crowded, impersonal world in which we live. In the noise and bustle of the present moment, when everybody seems to be engaged in frantic activity that often bears disturbingly meagre fruits, there is more than the occasional person who seeks desperately for someone simply to listen to him. A relationship of silent attention can in itself release emotional tension, and if it is enriched by understanding words, a new perspective may be given to the distraught person so that he can proceed on his way enlightened and at peace with himself and the world.

There is a difference between the knowledge that comes from scientific research into the various fields of human activity and the wisdom that is the fruit of deep human experience over the ages. Expert knowledge is invaluable in bringing us to a more complete understanding of the various problems that confront humanity, so that their causes may be dealt with as early as possible. But wisdom teaches us how to cope with the problem as it appears in our life. It focuses our thoughts on to less tangible realms of meaning and purpose; it sees life not only as an event to be experienced and enjoyed but also as an essential way towards growth into a full person. The counsellor therefore needs a comprehensive vision of life in which the various discordant aspects of existence can be assembled in a wider context, so that none need be dismissed as irrelevant or useless. The wise counsellor is always grateful for the understanding that the specialist can bring, but at the same time he remains mindful of the insights of the perennial wisdom that is the glory of the world's treasury of spirituality throughout all ages. To bring together the old and the new in creative tension is the work of wisdom at its highest.

To be an effective counsellor is to be open to the Holy Spirit. All who would know the counsel of the Holy Spirit must first submit in silent fortitude as they hear the truth about themselves as revealed by that Spirit. Then they can be silent in humility before the mystery of another person's life story. When ignorance is adorned with humility and given to God in devotion, the Holy Spirit penetrates the cloud of incomprehension and illuminates the dark places of the human personality with His radiance.

This book indicates how silent trust and openness to the wisdom of God can bring the counsellor close to his client, so that an understanding far greater than that deriving from human knowledge can lead all who are attentive on the path from fear and perplexity to truth, renewal and transformation. In the counsel that proceeds from the Holy Spirit the wisdom of God is aligned to His love, which we in turn give to those around us. A day's experience in the mighty roar of creation's thrust is more valuable to the counsellor than many years' reading of specialised texts. Our life story is our own precious book, and each new experience adds to its contents.

1.

The Way of the Spirit

The Spirit of God works deeply within us. He lifts up our consciousness from its natural attachment to ourself and our concerns to an atmosphere of infinite love that lies deeper in us than even the core of our own being. In other words, the Holy Spirit raises us far beyond the limitations of our own understanding so that we may drink deeply of the knowledge of God. Human knowledge bases its trust on the discoveries of science, and is the fruit of living experience throughout the ages of mortal endeavour. Divine knowledge flows to the receptive human soul in the practice of contemplative prayer, so that a completely new perspective is given to all that the mind had previously accepted as final truth. The understanding that comes from God is true wisdom; unlike the knowledge that is the fruit of human endeavour, it is broad, expansive, all-embracing and of transfiguring intensity. The knowledge that proceeds from man is discursive and analytical, and works best in categories of thought. It sees barriers rather than synthesis; it creates division, and exults when it has put everything into place. It likes to assume a dominant role, putting everything else into subjection to its own power.

But, in fact, there is one source alone of all knowledge, and that is God Himself. Were it not for the ceaseless activity of the Holy Spirit in the lives of men, their minds would fail to respond to the challenge of existence, and no fresh truth about the human condition would come to light and be the basis of a new understanding of the world and its workings. The Spirit of God never leaves us without His witness; He drives us on with a divine discontent that is the motivating force of all human creativity, whether artistic, scientific, philosophical or theological. The Spirit of God will never cease to grapple with the hard inertia of the human soul, longing above all else for indolent composure, until a new thing is born of its travail, until the virgin consciousness deep in the soul has conceived a greater truth and brought it into the light of common knowledge after a painful period of gestation. So the Spirit of God raises, by slow steps of disclosure, the purely human mind to spiritual illumination, bringing the separated soul into communion with all creation. This is the supreme gift of God to man; it determines the human spiritual nature and defines man's journey to completion, to a full participation in the divine reality.

The Spirit works best in a mind that is, at the same time, both empty of its own riches and yet also receptive to new truth. It is important in this respect to distinguish between mere mental passivity and alert mental receptivity. The passive mind lies inert, almost dormant. It may be too disinterested to be capable of assimilating any new information, or else it may be open indiscriminately to any external influence, so that it can become a channel for mischief and prejudice. Such may be the entranced mind that can be occupied and used by any invading psychic influence, whether from the living world or the world of the shades beyond death. In this world there move discarnate forms of those once with us in the flesh and also more subtle emanations from the psychic hierarchy of forms that are alternatively called angelic or demonic, depending on their source and activity. The passive mind is therefore the repository of indifferent influences arising from within the psyche of the person as well as from outside its immediate environs. In fact, there is a continuous, subtle interaction between what is within and what lies outside our consciousness. Taken in totality, the sensitivity of passive mental openness cannot be recommended as a desirable condition for authentic spiritual illumination; on the contrary, it is just as liable to be the source of delusion and false prophecy.

The state of mental receptivity, on the other hand, is one of watchful alertness, of active co-operation with the powers beyond one. In this state what is given is accepted for its own worth after being censored by the God-given rational faculty. The information received accords with the deeper intuitions of the soul, or true self, so that 'deep calls to deep in the roar of God's cataracts' (Ps. 42:7). Reason, intuition and aspiration are at once satisfied and fulfilled by the divine knowledge that enters an openly receptive mind; they are instructed and extended by a wisdom that enlarges the bounds of human understanding to a fuller dimension of awareness. When Jesus spoke to the common people, they listened eagerly (Mark 12:37), for they were astounded at His teaching; unlike the doctors of the law, He taught with a note of authority (Mark 1:22). The teaching of this obscure young man resonated with the aspirations deep in the souls of even His humblest listeners, whereas the conventional expositions of the law that they had heard before failed to penetrate beneath the superficial layers of the reasoning mind. They could agree with the words rationally, but they were secretly unmoved by what they had heard. The reason was that the teachers were themselves unchanged by the doctrine they preached; in fact it tended to isolate them from a full participation in the life of the community by enclosing them in a shell of complacency and self-esteem that separated them from their inner feelings and responses. This is what teaching that emanates from human sources so often does: it immures those who deliver the doctrine and those who accept it in a comfortable edifice of intellectual assurance. Here all problems and difficulties are reduced to a common denominator that can be manipulated by the mind, cut down to size, and then dismissed from further productive thought.

When the true prophet speaks, he gives utterance to the word of God that proceeds from his own soul but has its origin in the creative impulse that moves the whole cosmos. He is still, and enables God's word to use the experience of his life as a way of enlightening the minds of those who hear him. When the wisdom of God speaks through the human mouthpiece, that person is entrusted with adding his own contribution to the finished product. He does not alter the message, but flavours it with his own life's experience so that the supernatural wisdom is made available to the human audience through the prophet's own participation in the human condition. Without God there can be no true knowledge; without man that knowledge would remain unearthed and unformed. The human instrument brings the divine wisdom down to the capacity of his brothers. Their own souls are quickened by it, and a fresh view of reality is revealed to the people who have heard the message. From slothful apathy they are awakened to joyful commitment, so that in the end they may bear witness to an inner transfiguration of the human will that can now work in harmony and trust with God.

The receptive mind hears the divine message in that creative silence from which all virginal conceptions are brought through gestation to triumphant birth. The passive mind, on the other hand, is the indiscriminate channel through which any type of communication can proceed. Its end is delusion, so that those who hear its words are led astray into specious illusion and self-inflating reassurance. The Holy Spirit is the divine counsellor; from Him alone issues forth true counsel that renews the lives of those who are bowed down in tragedy and disillusionment. Only when the spirit of counsel shines through the lives and words of those who endeavour to help their fellow men, is light shed in the world's dark places and freedom granted to those who are in captivity to the limitations of the human condition. The world looks for comfort and rational solutions to problems, whereas the divine mind works towards transfiguration and the creation of a new society in which all are one in living relationship with each other and with God.

From all this it is apparent that the Holy Spirit imparts counsel best when the agent is in a state of rapt, self-giving contemplation. In this state his own personal desires are transcended – ultimately indeed to be broadened into a compassion that embraces all human suffering – so that he can transmit the message of God to those who seek help. The practice of contemplation is an essential element in an effective prayer-life – since contemplation is the way of approach of the soul to God as well as the end of the sequence of confession, petition and intercession that informs the soul's conversation with God. Until one can enter into rapt silence and surrender one's awareness in trusting love to the unknown ground of existence, one cannot effect a real communication with the Deity. But how can one carry out that sublime practice of contemplation in the heat of everyday encounter when silence is barely attainable and seen to be remote from one's consciousness? The secret is to practise the presence of God in all situations and on all occasions. If one is constantly aware of God's providence so that one is dedicating all one's thoughts, words and actions to Him, one is in effect contemplating Him. In a situation that requires urgent counsel one can call upon the divine presence at once and receive the power of the Holy Spirit. Words that are startling in their power then flow from one's lips, shaking one's preconceived ideas even as one kneels in the depth of self-effacement that is the prerequisite of a divine encounter. These are the words of truth appropriate to the situation in hand. If they are heard and inwardly digested, they can effect a revolution of spiritual renewal, and cause one to see the present dark way ahead in a completely different context.

The way to divine wisdom is through a confession of human ignorance. The way to God is by a path of unknowing when all that one had previously relied on proves inadequate, apart from a faith that persists despite all reason. And yet faith is dimly sustained by doubt and against doubt, as we shall see. As St Paul says, 'Divine folly is wiser than the wisdom of man, and divine weakness stronger than man's strength' (I Cor. 1:25). He goes on to remind his Corinthian disciples that they were of little account in the world's eyes in terms of wisdom or social advantage, yet to shame the wise God had chosen what the world counted folly, and to shame what was strong God chose what the world counted weakness. He had chosen things low and contemptible, mere nothings, to overthrow the existing order. And so there is no place for human pride in the presence of God (I Cor. 1:26–9). Pride is in essence an attitude of self-sufficiency that refuses to accept the free gift of love. It is not to be confused with self-esteem, which is a most important quality in all aspiring people and aims at preserving their lives and rendering them more fit to do the work that lies ahead of them. It becomes aberrant and destructive only when it exceeds its immediate mandate of self-preservation to do God's will and becomes an end in its own right. Then it uses other people for its own ends and becomes predatory and destructive to others and ultimately to the person also. By contrast, the proud person refuses to receive from another source, since he believes he embodies the fullness of wisdom. If the source is human he may be persuaded eventually to yield to its promises of greater knowledge to come. But if the source is beyond the rational faculty, on which most people pride themselves, he will not accept its gift until his pride is shattered by such a fall that he has at last been able to put the things of this world into proper perspective, neither denying their importance nor putting them on a divine pedestal.

The Holy Spirit is the true counsellor. He shows us what is to come and also gives us the strength to face the difficulties that lie ahead of us. Indeed He is both the strength and the giver, for only under His inspiration can we surmount the present impasse and be lifted on to a new plane of endeavour in which fresh possibilities provide an outlet for a new way of approach. We cannot rise to the full stature of a person until the Spirit is manifestly working in us. We cannot be of any assistance to anyone else until we are led by that divine Spirit. The work of counselling is, in effect, the way of transferring the power of the Holy Spirit from the counsellor to the client, from the minister of healing to the one in need.

The transference of psychic material from the analysand to his analyst is known to be a crucial releasing and healing mechanism in the work of deep psychotherapy. The phenomenon of transference is the heart indeed of all healing collaborations. We may believe that the use of

rational argument, intellectual debate and earnest exhortation is fundamental in setting a disturbed person on to a
proper course of action. But, useful as all this undoubtedly
is, it can be effective only when a deep rapport has been
established between the parties of the enterprise. And at this
stage, rational debate is often superfluous, since its tendency
and conclusion are immediately obvious to all who are
participating in the venture of inner healing. The divine
transfer is effected by the Holy Spirit who gives of Himself
to all who are open in receptivity and humble in self-regard.
'Come to me, all whose work is hard, whose load is heavy;
and I will give you relief. Bend your necks to my yoke, and
learn from me, for I am gentle and humble-hearted; and
your souls will find relief. For my yoke is good to bear, my
load is light' (Matt. 11:28–30). This text is spoken of Christ,
and the work of lightening the load is performed by the
Spirit that issues supremely from Him. That same Spirit
must issue from all of us who are to give counsel to the
distraught and minister healing to the disabled. We of
ourselves can do nothing that is ultimately helpful, although
it may seem impressive in the short term, but when we are
still and attentive, the power of God can work within us,
making use of our innate gifts and talents, so that we may be
the agents of deeds of such heroism and proclaim words of
such wisdom that lives may be changed as the result of our
ministry. This is the spirit of counsel that leads all in its
proximity to a full development of their potential as human
beings. The person who has the privilege of being used for a
counselling or healing ministry is especially sensitive to the
inspiration of the Holy Spirit, and remains alert to His
thrust and enlightenment at all times.

The human mind is beset with obstacles and limitations;
the spiritual mind can transcend the rational barriers of
what appears possible by entering upon new tracts of
exploration. This is the difference between a type of
counselling that is restricted to a particular theory of
personality development and integration and one that
admits its own ignorance and throws itself open to the divine
initiative. This type of ignorance is not to be confused with

obscurantism, an attitude that rejects all rational arguments and scientific developments, submitting itself totally to a sacrosanct tradition or a fundamentalistic regard for a sacred scripture. The ignorance of the human mind that can lead to its receiving divine wisdom is one of openness, humility and a deep-set sense of adventure into the unknown. The words of the One who sat on the throne of God and said 'Behold! I am making all things new' (Rev. 21:5) are also the words that come to all who truly counsel in the name of the Most High. They use the full armamentarium of modern science and understanding, but are also illumined by divine grace and inspired by the wisdom of the ages. In this way each personal problem is seen to be a unique event in its own right, and although bound to show a family resemblance to similar problems occurring in the lives of other people, it is nevertheless singular in its own emphasis and flavour, since it emanates from a particular, unique personality.

To be humble before the mystery of a fellow human being is the beginning of a genuine relationship with that person. To give of oneself in respectful silence to a person is to begin the work of counselling and healing, for in the tranquillity of self-giving, the Holy Spirit commences His work and a strengthening bond is effected between the one who serves and the one who is served. But that inner silence from which all good things are fed to those in need of help can dwell only in the person who has attained self-knowledge. When one can face and accept the areas of conflicting light and darkness within one's own psyche, only then can the Spirit of God use one in His healing work. As one transmits healing to others and words of counsel to the person in emotional confusion, so one is made a clearer and less obstructed channel for the work of the Holy Spirit and one attains a more effective inner cleansing of oneself. In this way there lies an authentic integration of the personality, one based on the all-seeing direction of God and not deflected by the biased, often one-sided theories of man. The end of the process is spiritual freedom, a freedom to serve God fully in one's own being and to attain divine understanding as the end of the process.

One cannot listen attentively to another person until one is at peace within oneself. A dialogue with oneself effectively excludes meaningful conversation with anyone else. If one is ill at ease in one's own depths, one will be in poor communication with all outside one. Only when one is deeply centred in the core of one's own being, which is called the soul or spiritual self, can one be available to hear the complaint of another person, and to flow out in silent attention to his needs. It is at this juncture that the Holy Spirit enters the conversation and sheds His healing grace upon the participants who are engaged in exploration of the depths of inner reality. Through His mediation there can be an exchange of psychic elements that is not only the heart of a true relationship between people but also the means of healing a broken personality.

2.

Illuminated Self-Love

Of one thing I have no doubt: until we can love ourselves there is no possibility of our loving anyone else, even a person as close to us in physical relationship as a parent, spouse or child. Only when we love ourselves with the intensity of charity that will accept all aspects of ourselves as infinitely treasurable, even when they are palpably immature if not frankly perverse, can we be still and flow out in charity to all around us. Love, as Jesus reminds us, if it is real should be bestowed on enemy as well as friend, just as our prayers of intercession if they are to be effective in changing people according to the will of God, must include those who treat us spitefully and whose attitude to us is disfigured with destructive jealousy. The ethical demands of Christ are indeed 'counsels of perfection', that there must be no limit to our goodness, as our heavenly Father's goodness knows no bounds (Mat. 5:43–8). The fruit of this goodness, the outer manifestation of which is love for all sentient creatures, indeed for all the creation of God, is an inner peace beyond human understanding. This peace in turn enfolds the beloved in an embrace that arises from God Himself and uses our feeble limbs and minds to bestow it on all our brethren. When I am at peace within myself, I am at peace with all the world, somehow being able to include all its contradictions and aberrations in a deep compassion that is the forerunner of a cosmic transformation. Certainly I cannot bestow counsel on anyone else until I am in such close rapport with him that I can give of my very essence to him. This is the prerequisite of any effective healing relationship, one in which the Holy Spirit can lead to a

sustained growth of the personality to the authenticity of
independence through the mediation of another person.

How can I know that peace that passes all human
understanding? It cannot be grasped or claimed, nor can it
be attained by an act of unaided will. The more it is strained
after, the further it recedes from my view; the more it is
coveted, the less does it lie within my field of attainment.
Peace is a gift of God, coming when one is least aware of its
necessity. For those who cannot accept the concept of deity,
I would say that as one yields oneself to the power that
energises life itself in simple trust, so one is filled with its
benevolence, and one is enabled to accept the present
situation in its potentialities as well as its threats for the
future. This may be the first experience of love in the life of
one who was previously agnostic about any power beyond
human understanding that could have a direct influence on
his welfare. Love that is real makes no demands on the one
to whom it is given. Inasmuch as the love that makes the
whole world move is bestowed equally on the good and the
bad, the receptive and those who do not respond, it arises
from a source that cares infinitely for all its creatures. Its joy
lies in witnessing the growth to maturity of what it has
created, the full outflowing of individuality in perfect
freedom of all to which it has given birth.

To love one's own infirmities is the first step in the healing
of those infirmities, which in turn shows us the way of the
spirit of counsel to those around us. Loving what is weak
and deficient within one is something that needs precise
definition. This love is not sentimental blurring of
distinctions of good and bad, nor is it a way of exonerating
oneself from personal responsibility by blaming one's
heredity or environment for one's defects. Neither is this love
a glamour-ridden narcissism in which one admires oneself in
rapt delight, seeing one's reflection in the pool of vain
imagination. Self-love is not to be equated with the
indulgence of our weaknesses in an orgy of liberal
permissiveness, in the same way as an ineffectual parent
would continue to indulge his wayward child instead of
teaching him the acceptable rules of conduct even, if need

be, through the infliction of effective punishment. 'My son, do not spurn the Lord's correction or take offence at his reproof; for those whom he loves the Lord reproves, and he punishes a favourite son' (Prov. 3:11–12). True love is to be contrasted with sentimental indulgence on the one hand and a concern for the world's opinion of oneself as a loving person on the other. Love that merits the strength of the word is strong, consistent in devotion, and enduring in intensity. It is a relationship in which one is prepared to part with something of supreme importance in one's life for another person's welfare. The most valuable gift any of us can so sacrifice to another is ourself, primarily in the form of our attention. When this is bestowed, undivided and unstinted, on a single human being, that person is brought into a creative relationship with ourself, even if the first emotions aroused are those of unease and distrust. Much inner aversion and resentment may have to be acknowledged before a real relationship can be established. True harmony is often the fruit of conflict that is patiently worked through in honest encounter. When we come to know another person in the depth of our own being, we start to love that person, since in the heart of inner regard the edge of surface identification is worn down and dispersed. There, adverse criticism, snobbish derision and intellectual arrogance fall away, leaving in their wake a deep affection that binds two vibrant people.

One cannot know this love for another person until one knows the secret of self-love: we love because He loved us first (I John 4:19). God loves us because He made us and even when we betray the divine image in which we were fashioned, the steadfast love of God does not fail. The love of God is bestowed equally on all His creatures, but whereas the good respond to that love and effect its circulation to all around them, the evil fail to accept the love and allow it to be dissipated heedlessly. Neither they nor anyone else can benefit from God's providence while they are in charge of the world's resources. But how can we know this love of God? When does it cease to be merely a theological abstraction and become a living reality? In many instances only when we have been brought so low that all the usual means of support have been irrevocably stripped from us. Then He who knocks perpetually at the door of the soul for admission can at last be heard, acknowledged and bade welcome. He was always there, but we were never available to attend: we had many more important matters in hand in the world of glamour than to spare the time to listen to the still, small voice within us.

In Jesus's greatest parable, that of the Prodigal Son (Luke 15:11–32), the boy who has spent all he possessed in reckless living comes to his senses, to his true self in fact, when he is in the most dire straits, at the point of absolute destitution. Then he hears the voice of God within him, telling him to confess the error of his ways to his father and offer himself as a paid servant. When, in fact, he arrives back home in the utmost humiliation, his father – far from rebuking him – runs out to greet him and take him to a feast of welcome. Nothing is too precious to be bestowed on the repentant son, 'for this son of mine was dead and has come back to life; he was lost and is found'. That is the paradigm of God's love for all who truly turn to Him in the secret place of the soul. It is tragic that the dutiful elder son feels no love at all, only a fully justified resentment of the festivities in honour of the return of the wastrel. He does not realise that he too is loved with an equal ardour for what he is. Until, however, he is open to the deeper springs of God's grace, the heavy cloud of his resentment cannot be dissipated by the rays of rejoicing that should attend the return home of a lost brother. It follows that God's love never fails, but that we have to be open to receive it. When it penetrates us, we are strangely free – free from past attachments and future fears, free from old resentments and fresh schemes for self-aggrandisement, free from the thralldom of past ways of thought and from bondage to the image that we had previously projected as part of our social identity. At last we can be ourselves without fear and without self-justification. No longer do we need to ingratiate ourselves with other people; no longer do we have to conceal our less pleasant qualities from the gaze of our fellows – which means, in effect, concealing them from our own gaze, since those around us are usually well aware of our inner disposition but are probably too self-engrossed or apathetic to care very much about it. Most of us have enough to cope with in our own orbit without becoming involved in another's problems except when they can help to relieve us of our sense of failure.

The love of God for each of us is His acceptance that we are as we are. This was the love Christ had for the prostitutes and sinners with whom He dined, obviously in an atmosphere of great rejoicing. He could see the craving for acknowledgment that lay deep within the apparently degraded personalities that showed themselves to the outer world in the form of immoral, vicious people. Inside there was a small child that had never been loved. Jesus loved the small child and, by the power of the Spirit of God, He brought that unprepossessing split-off part of the personality into full integration and maturity, so that the lust and greed of the unredeemed people around Him became transfigured into self-giving love and generosity to their fellows. We may be sure He did not preach repentance to them, for they would in all probability have rejected Him outright had He put himself in judgment over them. When they were accepted for what they were, the image of God – in which they too were created but which had been tragically distorted by the inroads of sin, both inherited and acquired – was restored to its original excellence. They were indeed born again, and yet nothing of the past was held in reproach or accusation. It was, as it were, their mark of identity and their reminder that they too had had feet of clay in the past. As Dame Julian of Norwich was shown, 'Sin is necessary, but all shall be well' (*Revelations of Divine Love*, chap. 27).

To love one's infirmities is therefore rather similar to loving one's small son or daughter even if it is a thorough nuisance to all in its vicinity. Such a child has to be educated into socially acceptable behaviour, as much for its own acceptance into the community as for the well-being of those around it. But it is never rejected or broken. It follows therefore that a psychological or moral weakness must first be accepted as a fact of one's inner life, and then offered up to God for healing in rapt prayer. For this prayer to be effective, the will to change must be active and fully committed. Thus there is no tendency to deny the magnitude of the infirmity or to play down its destructive role in the fulfilment of the person. But it is accepted without abhorrence and offered up to God for healing. In this process one becomes increasingly open to the infirmities of other people, and one can begin to flow out to them with a sympathy that may ultimately blossom into warm affection; the end is self-giving love, but this is the fruit of a lifetime's endeavour in the dark world of personal relationships, at once sordid and aspiring, treacherous and noble.

When I am, through my own sordid nature, separated in esteem from all my fellows, I am still loved by God. He is available to me in a way that was previously not possible owing to my own self-centred preoccupation with the things of this world. But when the world dissolves in a mist of unreality, the love of God remains and burns ever more brightly within me. I know I am healed by God's love when I am lifted up from the imprisonment of personal fears and insecurity to an awareness of the abiding providence of His grace, so that every part of my personality, the dark no less than the bright, is acceptable to me. This means, in other words, that when I have experienced God's love mystically, I can begin to accept myself as I now am. Then I can begin to practise the second great commandment laid down by Jesus, that of loving my neighbour as myself. As I am able to face the totality of my being, good and bad alike, so I am able to project my awareness into the people I meet in everyday life and to accept them for what they are, rather than for what I, in my arrogance, would have them be. Gradually destructive criticism gives way to a quiet acceptance, which in turn is succeeded by a strong, genuine admiration for the numerous good qualities I see in the souls of the people around me. The end-product is a love that is prepared to sacrifice itself for the other person's welfare. This is the true measure of love compared with which physical outpourings of emotion are mere superficial displays of affection. The greater the outpouring of love I show to others, the more complete is my own inner healing; in this way, the aberrations within me are cleansed, healed and finally transfigured into something of enduring value in my relationships with other people. The physician of the soul remains unhealed until he has brought all humanity into soul-consciousness. In the same way Christ remains in agony until the end of the world, as Pascal reminds us.

An inner healing relationship has a trinitarian foundation: God, myself and others. The greatest of these is obviously God, from Whom all blessings flow. But the central focus is oneself, on whom God acts in love and from whom love flows to those around. Without these there can be no effective circulation of love, and love cannot be returned fully to God. I love because I know the love of God. This love cannot remain sequestered within myself, because it is of the very nature of love to flow out to all creation. The outer manifestation of the Holy Spirit is love; all authentic gifts of the Spirit, as opposed to aberrant psychic manifestations, bring the word of God to the world. And the primary word of God is love. By love the world was created; by love it is sustained; by love it is redeemed from the bondage to selfishness (which is the core of sin) to enter into the full converse of God, the communion of all things in the divine image. The proof of this love, as St John's Gospel reminds us, is God's giving of His only Son, that everyone who has faith in Him may not die but have eternal life (John 3:16). It must be emphasised that the growth of the person into the knowledge of God's love, and hence into illuminated self-love and the love of the neighbour, is a life-long process. The saint is more aware of his lack of love than is the sincere atheist who may devote his life to social and political reform. As one grows in love, so one identifies oneself more completely with the publican in Jesus' central parable (Luke 18:9–14), who can say only 'Oh God, have mercy on me, sinner that I am'. Jesus himself was fully identified with sinners when He was nailed to the Cross between two of them. And in His love, He was able, in St Luke's account of the Passion, to redeem one of them from the cynical despair that ends the lives of most evil-doers, to an acknowledgment of the supremacy of spiritual values, as typified in Jesus Himself (Luke 23:39–43).

In this example of the lowliness of love, we gain fresh insight into the darkness of illuminated self-love. It sees in the very defects of the personality with which it has to grapple the face of God. Christ is often closer to the sinner than to the man of apparent virtue until he too sees his lack and gives himself wholeheartedly to his fellows. In the story of the rich young man who looks for the one thing needful to attain eternal life, Jesus tells him to give away everything he has, and then to follow him, a counsel impossible for the virtuous seeker after truth (Mark 10:17–22). In the story of the venal tax-gatherer, Zacchaeus, the healing of his moral defect by the love of Christ is followed by his voluntary disposal of the bulk of his money to charitable causes and his wholehearted reimbursement of anyone whom he had previously cheated (Luke 19:1–10). Zacchaeus had known the love of God in the course of his sordid preoccupation with money, and was thereafter disembarrassed of the need for money by the love of Christ. His life, including his ability to make money, was dedicated to God and to his fellow men.

The solution of this paradox of sin leading one to an encounter with God and apparent virtue separating one from Him lies in the nature of consciousness. Love is a function as well as a product of consciousness. The sinner, when he comes to a full knowledge of himself in the depths of dereliction, as symbolised by the prodigal son among the pigs, is open to the love of God in full awareness. At last he is in a position to acknowledge the one thing needful for his well-being. The conventionally righteous person, until even the fruits of his piety are put in their proper perspective, is separated from the greater love of God by his own moral rectitude, which shows itself in a failure to respond positively to the unclean, the sinner, the pervert and the criminal. And yet each of us contains these elements also in the deep unconscious part of the personality. Until they are acknowledged, loved and offered to God for healing, they will be projected on to those outside us whom we despise and fear most. The denial of love leads to rejection, and what is rejected tends to acquire a life of its own in the unconscious part of the psyche; the damage it is capable of causing is terrible. The twin monsters of our own century, fascism and communism, are too appalling a testimony to this truth to be ignored. In fascism the dark forces within the individual personality are projected on to vulnerable people of a foreign racial or religious origin. Among those attracted to communism the darkness of the self is aligned to the under-privileged masses so that it can be projected quite plausibly on to all who are successful and happy. These are identified with the rich exploiters of humanity. How often the virtuous impulse in religion has developed into a puritanical movement that has had its end in widespread persecution and destruction! Fascism and communism both have a powerful puritanical element that appeals to the self-righteous bigot in all of us, that uses the concept of God to destroy His works, that perverts moral rectitude to stifle the impulse of love and forgiveness. It was the Church of His time that conspired to crucify Jesus, not the common people around Him, who were weak rather than evil.

And yet we are not to indulge our weaknesses or those of other people. They are to be confronted, seen for what they are, and given to God in humble confession so that they may be healed. This is love in action; it is not simply a benevolent attitude but a way of life that works towards the healing of all things in God. Love is warm, but it has its chill also – for it demands everything we possess. Love endures all things, but it also works with impatience for the resurrection of folly to wisdom, for the maturing of selfish attitudes of juvenility to the self-giving sacrifice that crowns a life of creative experience. Self-love is no static ecstasy of self-approval. It is simply the first essential stage in an arduous re-creation of the personality into something of the fullness of the stature of Christ.

In the same way, only when we love the perversity that lies at the heart of another person's soul, can we effect a relationship with him. But the end of that relationship is a regeneration of that individual into a real person, one who has an alert, functioning will capable of choice, decision and action. Only when we have come to terms with the perversity within ourselves can we start to relate in earnest with the other person.

3.

Self-Discovery and Illumination

In the classical path of spiritual development as defined in the Catholic tradition, illumination stands in the middle of the purgative way that leads to union with God. In this way purgation, illumination and union are the sequence of the isolated soul's journey to participation in the knowledge of God, so that it may share in the very being of God (2 Pet. 1:4), in whose image it was, in the first place, fashioned and created. The isolation of the individual soul follows from its innate tendency to seek for itself in separation from living fellowship with anyone outside itself. This is shown by its absorption in its private interests to the exclusion of the wider claims of life. This is the state of sin that the world is perpetually facing: an isolation of living forms into monolithic units that cease to relate positively to anyone outside themselves, even using each other in a predatory fashion to realise the satisfaction of personal greed. The ego, that ever-changing focus of personal consciousness by which we identify ourselves and seek to assert ourselves in whatever situation we may find ourselves, soon becomes a bulwark of defence against any self-giving relationship with another person. Thus there is a state, if not of actual war, of at least armed neutrality between people that prevents self-giving openness in love. When this barrier to a full relationship is erected, the power of the Holy Spirit is seriously weakened in the lives of such entrenched personalities. The result is attrition of the full person and a movement from life to death.

It is an interesting observation that the aim of the psychotherapeutic process is to build up and establish an ego consciousness that can bring the individual into creative relationship with unconscious forces even of a dark type, and make him a person in his own right. By contrast, the way of the mystic is to transcend the claims of the ego and enter a new experience of personal identity that moves beyond material bondage, finding its end in union with God. This end might indeed be dismissed as an escape from the harsh realities of earthly life into an illusory absorption in the Absolute experienced as a state of impersonal non-existence. This is a description levelled by hostile, often ignorant, critics at some aspects of Eastern mysticism. In fact, this is a travesty of the state of absorption into the divine that characterises the spiritual experience of the truly illumined Hindu or Buddhist saint. The reason why the end of authentic mystical illumination is not simply an elevated transcendence of the earthly condition is because union with God brings with it, as an inevitable consequence, union with all life. This includes primarily fellowship with all people. In this way alone can be obeyed Jesus' two fundamental commandments: the absolute love of God and the love of neighbour as of self. The first necessarily incorporates the second; the second is ultimately impossible without the first, though it might appear as a transitory atheistic phase of goodwill based on shared intellectual concepts. It could never embrace all people, however, let alone all life unless God were the centre of the love.

And yet the psychotherapeutic concern for the liberated self, manifest as the ego in everyday relationships, and the mystical rejection of the isolation of the ego, which is seen to be an illusion, have features in common and are not necessarily antagonistic. In the end what matters is the nature of the self by which identification is attained. To know oneself as an independent focus of consciousness that responds to a definite name and has a purpose in life is the beginning of one's identity, and around it forms the personality we experience inwardly and project outwardly to the world around us. There are, alas, many people who have not attained that degree of integration necessary for them to identify themselves as special individuals in their own right. The experience of separate identity that normally dawns on one in very early childhood should be substantiated and confirmed by the acceptance from one's parents, family and, finally, one's peer group that one receives during the years of growth up to adulthood. To this ought to be added one's achievements in the fields of scholarship and athletics that should punctuate one's life at school and then possibly at a place of higher education. In this way we can experience ourself as a unique person in whatever situation we find ourself by the time we have become an adult. In this growth towards the identity of a fully established person, the outer focus of which is the ego-consciousness that we identify with ourselves, two requirements must be met: the acknowledgment of one's peers and the love of one's family on the one hand and an assured place in society on the other. This assured social position is dependent on the work we do, the satisfaction we gain from it, and the recognition that accrues as a result of its achievements. People who are accepted with love by those closest to them, and have a secure position in the society around them, are well set to having a full awareness of their identity, and then being able to actualise it in the world in which they function.

On the other hand, the person who has never been acknowledged while yet a child and whose social roots are tenuous and unsatisfactory will have a poor sense of personal identity. He will tend to be taken over by outside forces stronger than himself, and also be dominated by inner impulses and emotions that have never been fully acknowledged and assimilated in his childhood. Among these invidious psychic charges are fear based on insecurity, resentment that one has been cheated out of the affection that was one's due, hatred of others, especially the foreigner and stranger who would appear to threaten one's existence, and a nebulous sense of meaninglessness in life, so that death and annihilation seem a more acceptable solution to existence than does the hard, loveless face of everyday life. If such an individual is to be healed, to be brought into full communication with his unconscious mind and established as a complete person, an ego-consciousness has to be fashioned from the vapid elements of his inner life.

And yet the ego that is dependent on outer acknowledgment is an uncertain, fluctuating centre of awareness. If it is not substantiated by something greater than material achievement, more enduring even than deep personal relationships, it will wither as the person grows old. With the process of ageing, the landmarks of earlier life become dim; their façades are obliterated by the inroads of time and oblivion. Decay marks the place where once a living monument to man's ingenuity stood proud and erect. There is in all of us, if we begin to know ourselves fully, a deeper focus of identity that transcends the claims and prizes of this mortal life and sees meaning in an existence far greater than anything we may know in purely rational consciousness. To gain access to this seat of transcendental knowledge there may have to be a complete surrender of all that was previously held inviolable and sacrosanct. It is the pearl of great price that, once found, demands a complete sacrifice of all else we possess before it can be claimed as our own. As Jesus told those who were disciples,

> Anyone who wishes to be a follower of mine must leave self behind; he must take up his cross and come with me. Whoever cares for his own safety is lost; but if a man will let himself be lost for my sake and for the Gospel, that man is safe. What does a man gain by winning the whole world at the cost of his true self? What can he give to buy that self back? (Mark 8:34-7).

The self that has to be left behind is the ego-consciousness with all its assurance and glory as well as its defilement and corruption. The safety we care for is the identity we cling to with its rich rewards of wealth and reputation. Indeed, our reputation is hardest of all to surrender, since on it depends our standing in the world's eyes and the security that follows from it. But if our very identity is sacrificed for the highest we know, the word of God that inflames the depths in us, we gain an identity that is proof against all the winnowing fire of the world's hatred, fickleness and destructive jealousy.

This identity is heavenly and no longer subject to the vicissitudes of mortal life and death. It can never be taken from us, for once we live by it, the whole world is seen to be an insubstantial pageant, and all its prizes futile as compared with the one thing needful for eternal joy. This is the deep centre within that is in everlasting fellowship with God, since God Himself has taken His place in its holiest point. This teaching is essential to the mystical understanding of all the great religious traditions and is the path trodden by all their saints. It is not acquired by study so much as by the journey of life itself. On it depends man's place as the agent of God in the working of this world. Until an individual knows of this truth and starts to live by it – no easy matter, let it be said at once – he has not arrived at a fully human stature, and therefore cannot be a satisfactory counsellor to those still groping for inner identity.

The stage on the spiritual path described as illumination is an experience of the presence of God which has its fruit in enlightening the responses of the person to a completely new understanding of reality. Whereas previously reality was understood in purely rational, materialistic terms related to personal survival and procreation, it is now grasped as a dimension, an atmosphere (all words fail to do it full justice) of love, meaning and assurance that brings all earthly endeavours into eternal significance. The meaning I speak of is that all mortal experiences, good and bad alike, have their end in building the personality to something that far exceeds the inevitable selfishness of the isolated ego-consciousness (inevitable because of its attachment to survival), and the assurance that full personhood will be attained at the end of life's struggle. In this illumined state the glory of a realised person is seen to transcend the barrier of physical death, and the attainment of this state of being is a presage of, indeed a preparation for, immortality. The illumined person therefore knows something of the eternal life in God even as he treads the weary path of mortal existence, and is able to bring some promise of this eternal life in his endeavours to all those around him. This he does not by description, let alone exhortation, but by his very presence and the healing atmosphere he brings with him in his silence as much as in his speech and actions. It seems to me that no counsellor can attain the fullness of his remedial work until he is vouchsafed a further vision of the destiny of humanity as a whole than the very limited view available to those around him. It is to the one with at least partial sight that is entrusted the privileged work of leading the blind.

The obvious danger of this approach is that the person who claims special illumination and is boosted up egoistically by his 'revelation', will be encouraged to assume the exalted mantle of the master, the initiate, or the guru, according to the tradition he adopts. He will lead others by way of his private opinions, obligingly substantiated by visions and inner voices of authority, which are far more likely to be dangerous delusions than authentic beacons on the path of self-realisation and world service. In no field of human endeavour is the scriptural injunction to test the spirits more essential:

> But do not trust any and every spirit, my friends; test the spirits, to see whether they are from God, for among those who have gone out into the world there are many prophets falsely inspired. This is how we may recognise the Spirit of God: every spirit which acknowledges that Jesus Christ has come in the flesh is from God, and every spirit which does not thus acknowledge Jesus is not from God. This is what is meant by 'Antichrist'; you have been told that he was to come, and here he is, in the world already (I John 4:1–3).

The Spirit of God is revealed in Christ, by His work of healing, humility and self-sacrifice in the world for the redemption of sinful humanity. He took nothing for Himself – whether money, credit for His works or power to dominate the political scene; He gave everything to humanity in the name of the Father from Whom He acknowledged all gifts and power. He said, for instance, to Pilate 'You would have no authority at all over me if it had not been granted you from above' (John 19:11). The truly illumined person leads by a light far greater than anything he can muster from his own imagination. Nor can it be created by the manipulations of the intermediate powers that inhabit the psychic dimension of reality. It is the light of God, uncreated and of an intensity of brightness far beyond the comprehension of the naked human intelligence. This is the manifestation of true sanctity, the seal of Christ, Who is the light of the world. He is also the way, the truth and the life (John 8:12 and 14:6). Though beyond human attainment, the light comes to all who are capable of receiving it, and in it lies the assurance of ultimate purpose even in the impenetrable darkness of prevailing doubt and despair at their most urgent and acute.

The illumination that comes from God is an important phase in self-discovery. It confirms that there is a true identity in all of us that will outlast the vicissitudes of this mortal life and is of the nature of Christ within, our personal hope of glory to come as well as the greater promise of healing for all humanity. This peak of illumination is, in fact, the experience that mystics have in their journey to communion with God. It cannot be grasped or manipulated, since attempts to reproduce the effect with drugs deprive the person of the sharp intellectual discrimination that is necessary to understand what has been given and the moral dedication to use it for the benefit of the world. Illumination, however, need not always come as a cataclysmic event that completely changes one's perspective; even St Paul's dramatic conversion experience on the road to Damascus was in all probability the zenith of the climax of a spiritual revolution that was slowly and unobtrusively taking place within him. It is unfortunate that the 'peak experience' is often taken out of its proper context as an indication of the way lying ahead of the person to the full actualisation of his unique being as a child of God, and made a thing to be grasped in its own right, so that it may comfort and exalt the individual, making him feel in some way special and remote from his fellow men.

When the deeper reality of the soul, the true or spiritual self, is known, its radiance penetrates the whole personality. Then the ego-consciousness, instead of being annihilated, is lifted up to the spiritual self within, and indeed it becomes an external focus of the self that is one's true identity. Thus the statement of John 10:30 that the Father and Christ are one, finds its attainment in all people who have been given a direct knowledge of the presence of God within them. Certainly in Jesus the Father is constantly revealed, something that cannot be said for even the greatest saint in the world. Nevertheless, the person living a life of spiritual radiance shows his inner identity to the world, and his life is no longer merely his, but that of Christ living in him (Gal. 2:19). The ego is the very mirror of the soul in a spiritual person. In him the ego is no longer a bellicose, rather childish focus of self-assertiveness that acts as an effective barrier against a full communication with the unconscious depths within the personality. Instead it becomes the open road that leads to the spirit within a person.

In the same way the illumined ego can be still and silent before both God and man. It can then receive the full impact of divine wisdom as well as the hesitant, often painful information that flows from the depths of a fellow human being. To be a minister of God's counsel, that is the privilege as well as the responsibility of working in full openness to the Holy Spirit, one must therefore be at peace with oneself and focused in the centre of one's true being, the soul or the spiritual self. In that heavenly stillness one may be given words of supernatural wisdom, even if one flinches in one's humble intellectual status before the judgment of the mighty of this earth. These inner words may completely alter one's life and the lives of others around one.

To give counsel is the act of an intermediary, indeed an intercessor, between God and man. The aim of the work of counselling is seldom to give clear directives; it is primarily to be a silent channel through which God's wisdom can be transmitted to the human mind. The most profound communication takes place between two people who care so deeply for one another that they can relate perfectly in a silence that is wordless and yet eloquent in content. As one explores the depths of one's inner being, so one encounters the soul which is the centre of integration of the whole personality. From that centre one can flow out in fellowship to anyone who is able to listen and participate in the conversation; the person in need of guidance is especially open to that communication. Furthermore, the Spirit of God that joins us all together in one body has a healing purpose that is independent of the knowledge of the minister of healing, and a cogency that is more powerful than even the most studied advice which might be uttered by a trained counsellor relying on technical understanding alone.

Where the Spirit of the Lord is, there is liberty (2 Cor. 3:17). The seat of wisdom is the centre of the soul called the spirit of man; this is in direct communion with the Holy Spirit, Who dwells in all of us, since He is the Lord and giver of life. Whereas in the other animals He acts as a power that cannot be responded to in a rational way, in the human being He can be accepted, heeded and obeyed with joy and thanksgiving. The truly spiritual person has a conscious awareness of divine things that is lacking in the one who is unspiritual. And let it be said at once that spirituality is independent of intellectual attainment. On the other hand, an innate spirituality is greatly cultivated and strengthened by the disciplined development and use of the rational mind. The great mystics have all been people of considerable under-standing and intelligence, but their wisdom far transcended the learning contained in books. On the other hand, it did not impugn the truth of Holy Scripture but rather elucidated it and fulfilled it in the art of illumined living.

The spirit of man is the centre of being from which all spiritual gifts take their origin, at least in respect of the person himself. In this centre, the Holy Spirit can show Himself to us and speak with an unclouded and uncoloured directness. His word is then free from the distortion that invariably disturbs His discourse when He speaks through the mind of someone who is sullied with prejudice or fear. In this way fear, concern for one's own standing in the world, and distrust of other people and their way of life can seriously interfere with, and even prevent, the full flow of counsel from the lips of the one who is entrusted with the word that heals. On the other hand, if one is properly centred, the Holy Spirit will give one that inner freedom to speak the inspired word and proclaim the presence of God, from Whom all healing and counsel proceed. The responsibility is shared between God and man. Our part in the transaction is to be as perfect in love and service as lies within our reach. This requirement would be all but impossible were it not for the indwelling Spirit of God who leads us, when we are obedient to His voice, from the bondage of either egoistic selfishness or crippling self-denigration to the experience of all-embracing grace. In this healing experience of God's grace the word brings a new perspective to all who listen.

The secret is constant openness to God at all times and places, so that each event, indeed each person, though apparently well known and documented in the past, is now seen with fresh eyes that discern an unaccustomed radiance in the common round of life. This openness to the divine is assuredly a gift of grace, but is also a way of life. As one gives of oneself in unremitting service to the world, so one renders oneself more open to the love of God, Who in turn uses one for further service. The recompense for that service is the harvest of the spirit, described by St Paul in Galatians 5:22 – love, joy, peace, patience, kindness, goodness, fidelity, gentleness and self-control. This amazing harvest is not given simply to be accumulated for the benefit of the one who has received the blessing; it forms the basis of a life of further self-giving, the end of which is the bestowal of a similar harvest on as many other people as are able to receive the blessing. No genuine spiritual gift, nor the harvest of spiritual living, can possibly remain hidden or sequestered in the life of a person who has given up himself to God's service. The end of God's work is universal healing, so that all creatures may be redeemed from the slavery of personal attachment (which in the human being is the basis of sin). All who love God work ceaselessly for the reclamation of that which is lost, for the transfiguration of all that is at present unclean and corrupt.

This is the end of the experience of illumination and marks the point of full self-discovery. We are all parts of one universal body, and the self is never entirely enclosed in or limited by the single physical body that we call our own and that responds to the name given it at the time of our birth into this world.

4.

The Path of Counsel

The path of counsel is the way of life that leads to the encounter with the wisdom of God's Spirit. That Spirit, as we have already seen, lies within us, and the attainment of His knowledge is God's gift to us. But we have to be perpetually ready to receive this summons, lest the pearl of great price remains unobserved and therefore unclaimed. The spirit of counsel is intimately related to the spiritual self that is our true identity, were we only in conscious relationship with it. As we have already noted, the identity we know and seek to preserve is a narrowly egoistical one based on such superficial appurtenances as age, sex, social and financial position and intellectual attainment. These find their summation in the role we play in the world around us, and their outer manifestation constitutes the image of ourselves that we project on to others and take refuge in when we are alone and our faith is sorely tried. In itself this is not so much reprehensible as childish, for that identity not only fluctuates in the short-term but is also irreversibly diminished by the inroads of time and ageing, disease and degeneration, and finally death with its apparent end of all mortal endeavour. As St Paul says 'If it is for this life only that Christ has given us hope, we of all men are most to be pitied' (1 Cor. 15:19). The counsel that proceeds from the egoistical person, even if he is replete with the latest psychological knowledge, will be dominated by his own opinions and view of life. He cannot avoid, by the very frailty common to us all, taking the higher seat and assuming the master role. Therefore his counsel is of man's knowledge rather than of God's wisdom. It will consequently tend to be biased and even at its more brilliant will lack the perception that comes from the burning intuition of the naked soul. This is where the deeper, more comprehensive identity of the person resides, and it makes itself felt more keenly as we move on the path of life. Here our opinions are constantly being challenged by new data, and the rather superficial criteria of our identity are being ground down in the attrition that age and experience bring in their wake.

How does one encounter this spiritual self which is the foundation stone of our personalities, the rock on which our being is exquisitely fashioned? The most compelling recognition occurs in the infused mystical experience which changes our entire view of life, but this experience comes by the grace of God. If it is in any way fostered or cultivated, either by drugs or by special meditation techniques, it is sullied and cheapened. If it is captured it is degraded into an egoistical possession, tending to exalt one's innate selfishness so that one believes one is the repository of a special knowledge and therefore a very remarkable person. If it is given by God, it regenerates the personality and becomes the centre around which the new man is born and gradually develops into a real person. He is emphatically himself and none other, but now the integrating power is no longer the predatory ego but the person of Christ Himself. We have met St Paul's doctrine already: 'I have been crucified with Christ: the life I now live is not my life, but the life which Christ lives in me' (Gal. 2:19). Christ does not 'take over' the life of the person whose being He has entered as a conscious presence. He instead illuminates it with meaning and purpose, so that the innate qualities of that person are made manifest and the gifts of the Holy Spirit allowed to play their proper role in his future work for his own development as well as the benefit of those to whom he ministers.

It is in the practice of inner silence that the true self is known and its fountain of living wisdom encountered and tapped. Silence in this respect is an attitude of inner stillness in which there is practised awareness, attention, and deep concern for other people in addition to one's own need. The practice of *awareness*, or alert mindfulness, is one in which the senses and mind are open and receptive to all information that impinges itself on them. This information comes as sensory stimuli and also as intuitive shafts of understanding that appear to arise from the very depths of one's being. Each stimulus and the emotion it evokes are acknowledged without prior judgment, whether it is good or bad, beneficial or malign. It is the phenomenon itself that is significant, and the emotion that accompanies it reveals much about ourselves and our most intimate reactions to our inner life as well as the world around us. This awareness of one's present disposition and the emotions that arise within one are not to be confused with morbid introspection, in which one's attitudes and actions are analysed and deliberated upon in minute detail to the detriment of the present place of work and the needs of those around one. The aware person is inwardly still and quiet, being in proper relationship with his own psyche while at the same time participating freely in the world around him. In this state of self-awareness the barrier that usually separates the inner life of the person from the life of the world around him is thinned until it is finally breached. It was said of Christ that at the moment of His death the curtain of the temple was torn in two from top to bottom (Mark 15:38); in that death the sacred and the profane were finally united, and through that death and what followed we too can effect a union between the inner temple of the soul and the world outside when we are aware of the sanctity of all life concentrated in the present moment, which is unique in content and can never be repeated.

Attention follows awareness. It means a focusing of our awareness on a particular person or phenomenon. Attention is a total giving of oneself to the situation around one, and brings with it discernment and commitment. Our attention is the most immediately useful part of ourselves that we can give to anyone, but it is valuable only when it is pure, undivided and tranquil. This purity and fullness of attention can be known only to a person who is at peace in himself and has learned the lesson of enlightened self-love. When we need no longer flinch at any revelation concerning ourselves, then we are free to contemplate another person, or a more complex event, with wholehearted commitment. The special equanimity that allows us to accept whatever is in store for us in trust, since we have moved beyond the need for assurance and recompense for what we have done, also enables us to give of ourselves fully in psychic outflow to another person.

Concern crowns awareness and attention. It is a positive psychic relationship between one person and another in which the one can share in the unhappiness and distress of the other. The end of this relationship is a positive action to relieve the distress. In some situations this may entail an outer response of help, but more often all that can be done is to vow an inner commitment to that person's needs. This commitment shows itself in holding him in one's thoughts and praying regularly for him. The inner link is strengthened by the more material communication afforded by the telephone and the welcome visit. And yet the concern should always be non-attached. One is not there to take over the life of another person or even to influence it in a particular spiritual direction. This is the work of God's Spirit in a person's life. But when one is infused with the spirit of counsel, one can assist the Holy Spirit working in that person by being available and also acting as a mouthpiece of wisdom when the time is opportune. This requires a sensitivity of response that is beyond the reach of the naked human consciousness, for we tend to rush in all too often because we feel the need to justify ourselves or our opinions. But the spirit of counsel cleanses and enlightens the intuition, and affords shafts of the most penetrating insight into the disposition of the person in pain. It is then that the appropriate word flows from the mouth of the counsellor, who himself acts as a purified instrument of God's peace and does not need or attempt to assert his presence with lordly advice.

It is in the silence of losing oneself in concern for someone in distress that one finds oneself as one really is. When one's commitment is total and one's inability to ease the situation by rational means is equally complete, one enters a dark silence in which there echoes a shattering awareness of impotence both in being of help to anybody and, more starkly, in being true to oneself in the depths of one's present inadequacy. When we can no longer act constructively, at least according to our own judgment of what is a helpful response, we are cast over the precipice of self-esteem that we ourselves had erected. We hurtle downwards, dashing ourselves against the jutting rocks of submerged unconscious complexes that more usually reveal themselves to us in dreams of which the main features and trends are represented as symbols. When we reach the bottom, bruised and diminished in our self-esteem and enveloped in a dark world of menacing images that often take their origin from the earliest period of our life, a light shines distantly before us. It is the light of the world, the Christ within each of us. As we move by hesitant, rationally unguided steps towards that light, we find that it too is moving towards us when our inner disposition is directed by willed self-discipline and service to others. When the light meets us, or more precisely when we have entered into the light by arduous yet fearful steps into the unknown, that light affords us the key to our own identity, and what is revealed puts any previous comprehensive view of the world into imbalance and disarray.

The light is surrounded by silence, indeed is the very heart of the silence. The more in fellowship one is with one's true being, the more emphatic, embracing and invigorating does the silence become. To be outside the orbit of the silence becomes intolerable, and indeed eventually an impossible situation, because from the silence issues forth the Word of God in Whom alone is life. As a result one is always accompanied by the silence of inner peace, and is attended by its invariable fruit of deep communion with the soul of any person one is called on to meet and assist. Thus the disciplined silence of a life of prayer on behalf of others has its ultimate fruit in the attainment of a free, joyous silence in which one flows out in blessing to all around one.

This silence would seem, at least as an unqualified state, to be one of isolation from the world and a determined withdrawal from the company of those around one. In fact this aspect of silence is only the preliminary discipline that points to a much deeper, fuller and more committed way to communication with all kinds of people, and not only those whom one likes or with whom one shares some special interest that brings the participants together in a private, exclusive enterprise. In the silence of the true self that is also a focus of God's uncreated light by which His emergent energies are known to His creatures and made available to them, we enter a common unity of knowledge and regard. It is said of Christ that when even two or three are gathered together in His name, He is in the midst of them (Matt. 18:20). To be gathered together in Christ's name means to be bound together in His nature, inasmuch as the name of a person is the way by which we enter into a knowledge of his unique identity. It is for this reason that we cannot give a finite name to the Ultimate Source of Being from Whom all creation stems. The title god can be applied to any individual source of free will, and as such is used biblically even in respect of leaders and judges who are invested with god-like powers over those subject to them, but fail to execute these powers with love and justice (Pss. 58:1 and 82:1, 6). God the Father, on the other hand, works according to the way His nature was perfectly revealed in the ministry of Christ. In the same way, the name and nature of Christ are with all who enter into the silence of prayer in service to those who are in pain and mental agony. Furthermore, that silence of deep inner commitment to all who are in need of reassurance and love flows out in a never-abating stream from the one who lives and speaks from his inner depths where the true self is encountered and emits a perpetual radiance.

It follows therefore that the initial withdrawal from the world and the necessary inner retrenchment to find, establish and speak from the true self is fructified by bestowing the sacred quietness of the self on all whom one meets in everyday life and especially on those to whom one ministers healing and counsel. The silence of the self, far from making us remote from the world and separating us from our fellows, is the bond that the Holy Spirit uses to effect intimate spiritual relationships for the healing of many people. In the silence we are able to imbibe freely of God's wisdom and also the psychic obfuscation and emotional turmoil that may be around a person in great mental agony.

Once the silence has been experienced – and, as I have already indicated, it usually comes to one as an inner revelation during great suffering or at the peak of an intense emotional or aesthetic experience, although there are some unusual people who have known the inner silence of divine communion from their earliest years and have never been deflected from its sanctity despite the claims and temptations of the world – it has to be guarded, nurtured and made available to others. This is where the life of spirituality is vitally important. This life has been preserved and propagated in all the world's authentic religious traditions, Western and Eastern alike, that see the end of humanity in sharing fully in the divine nature, which is both personal in relationship to the finite individual and transpersonal in relationship with the cosmic flow with which the human mind grapples by transposing it into categories of time and space. It must be emphasised that the nature of reality is never impersonal, for personality is life and love, and as such it is lavished on all creatures equally, irrespective of their apparent usefulness to society. 'The kind of religion which is without stain or fault in the sight of God our Father is this: to go to the help of orphans and widows in their distress and to keep oneself untarnished by the world' (Jas. 1:27).

The concern for those who are helpless follows from an attitude of harmlessness to all life. Being unsullied by the world is not to be interpreted as an other-worldly withdrawal from participating in the common round of everyday living, still less a despising of the joys inherent in the full use of the body and its senses. Every aspect of earthly life can lead to an encounter with the divine were our awareness sharpened to the keenness of immediate recognition and response. Where the temptation of the world emerges as a constant threat is in our selfish, predatory attitude to its beauty and riches. As soon as the natural, predatory ego-consciousness takes control, it seeks to acquire, hoard and control the world's resources for itself. There follow from this selfishness of intent the evils of greed, dishonesty, jealousy and hatred which culminate in strife between people and ultimately war between nations.

The way in which one can play one's proper role in worldly society without becoming entangled in its muck and slime is by entering fully into an authentic spiritual tradition that has as its points of reference a sacramental life observed in fellowship by all who strive for better faith, the assiduous practice of prayer, and a deep awareness of personal inadequacy in the face of the divine love. This renders confession a necessary daily observance with its end in the full absolution accorded by a God whose nature is always to have mercy. The warmth of His love embraces in forgiveness even the most terrible sinner once he has repented and strives towards a new life of penitence in service and sacrifice of self for his brothers. To those who cannot accept the divine presence as a personal power that can absolve sin directly, a compromise can be struck by accrediting to the cosmic process itself the power to heal that which is aberrant and seeks a fresh start. In due course the love that informs this process will make itself a very real presence in the heart of the seeker, so that he will be aware that the power which moves the universe is in him also, and is constantly aware of his need and responsive to his entreaty.

The things of ultimate reality are not tractable to the natural, unaided reason, but as one grows in spiritual experience, so the natural reason – which is never to be denigrated, let alone disregarded – is imbued with divine grace and is able to attain an understanding of eternal truth. The phenomena of this world, far from being the sum of all truth, are simply the surface of what we call reality. While not in themselves illusions, as some mystical traditions would imply, they are in essence outer, visible signs of a reality that is hidden from our natural senses and of spiritual intensity. In other words, to the person imbued with vision all the world is a sacrament, and nothing that occurs in his life is devoid of a deeper, spiritual content that leads him closer to the source of all life, whom men call God. This applies, to those with openness and humility, equally to the agreeable and the unpleasant experiences of life. All are here to teach us not to cling to any present security, but to see our lives as expendable, being offered as a perpetual sacrifice for the world. It is only in this frame of mind that we can escape from the bondage of the ego-consciousness to the freedom of full identity, by which alone there is a complete participation in life. Then we know the truth which sets us free (John 8:32). This truth is shown in the revelation of Christ, Whose presence is the eternal spirit of the soul. He sets us free from the clinging necessity for constant recognition and recompense. Indeed, if the Son sets you free, you will indeed be free (John 8:35). And in the freedom of the soul, the spirit of counsel speaks with a clarity and an authority that bring new life to all who hear the word and pursue the doctrine in action and dedication.

The practice of prayer is the most important inner work on the path to sanctification. By prayer there can be an encounter with the world's grime that leaves one untarnished and the world a cleaner place for one's presence in it. In the dedicated silence of giving oneself wholly to God, the Holy Spirit (before, an unacknowledged presence in our life) now makes Himself heard inwardly and accepted joyously in the depth of our being. Since the spirit of counsel is a gift of the Holy Spirit, it reveals itself best when the mind is completely open in willed assent to the workings of God within it. The gift of the Spirit that seems to be especially close to the spirit of counsel, according to St Paul's list in 1 Corinthians 12, is the one of putting the deepest knowledge into words. This is the second of the list; the first, described as the gift of wise speech, can also be included. St Paul says in 1 Corinthians 2:11–13,

For the Spirit explores everything, even the depths of God's own nature. Among men, who knows what a man is but the man's own spirit within him? In the same way, only the Spirit of God knows what God is. This is the Spirit that we have received from God, and not the spirit of the world, so that we may know all that God of His own grace has given us; and, because we are interpreting spiritual truths to those who have the Spirit, we speak of these gifts of God in words found for us not by our own human wisdom but by the Spirit.

In prayer it is the Holy Spirit Himself Who is the initiator of the act as well as its final consummation. He tells us of our lack and our need for confession when we are silent enough to hear His voice inside us. And when we have confessed our sins and made our petition to ourselves in clear consciousness, in the presence of God, with rededicated lives and a determined will to do better in the future, the Spirit sheds His healing radiance on to the troubled soul, and starts a new phase of life within. Each day we tend to relapse into the shoddy unconcern for truth that typifies the world around us. Each day the spirit of prayer raises us from the all-encompassing quagmire of indifference to a peak of aspiration in which the whole universe is transfigured in light and raised up to a fresh vision of glory. It is in this state of awareness that the spirit of counsel flows most perfectly from our lips, purifying our lives and giving peace to all those around us. It is no wonder then that the path of counsel is illuminated by shafts of prayer. These form the foundation of each day's work, and are also constantly on our lips as we ask for guidance in a difficult situation. This situation need not necessarily concern oneself directly. In the work of counselling it is the other's problem that is the focus for guidance, and once again, the spirit of counsel issues forth in the word of the person who is in prayer even while at work.

It must be emphasised, however, that prayer is no substitute for technical knowledge, and the treasury of understanding with which we have been blessed from the insights of the acknowledged masters of psychology is not to be laid on one side and forgotten. On the other hand, it is to be used with a grateful yet astute discernment. The spirit of counsel enables one to make use of all the means at one's disposal to help another person in difficulties. But now these remain the means in hand and do not become so dominant as to form an end in themselves. The end is always the growth of the individual into a full person who can assume responsibility for his life and his actions under the guidance of the divine power within him. The spirit of counsel is the word which delivers all who are attentive from the slavery of unconscious attitudes of the past to an active participation in the life of the present. The word does not dominate, still less dictate, the way of future life. It acts instead by releasing the potential for growth in the one who is open, so that the point of integration within him who hears is now awakened and active. It is from this centre of authenticity that the new life is directed, a life at once precarious and assured of consummation.

The path of counsel is the life of disciplined awareness of the present moment. 'If your eyes are sound, you will have light for your whole body' (Matt. 6:22). As the aspiring athlete gears every muscle for the contest before him, sacrificing the temptations of the flesh for the greater prize ahead, so the one who treads the path of counsel learns to sacrifice all paltry diversions for the privilege of attending to the word within him which speaks of eternal life. The beacons on this path are self-giving *service* to others, an inner life of *prayer* and devotion to the Most High, and *awareness* of the deeper meaning inherent in even the most trivial circumstances of everyday existence.

5.

Bearing One Another's Burdens

The heart of an authentic creative relationship between two people is the ability of the one to share in the keenest intimacy the burdens that afflict the other. In fact, there can be no deep, enduring relationship with anyone else until one is in right relationship with oneself, especially the darker layers of the unconscious with its menacing shadow figure that epitomises all the hidden, subterranean powers within oneself that have a destructive tendency until they are brought into the light of full consciousness. Then these dark forces can be transfigured and allowed to play their proper role in one's psychic life. A transparent relationship with the less agreeable but very important parts of our own psyche is possible only in intimate communion with God, Who is at once immanent in the spirit of the soul and transcendent of all human knowledge and imagination. The proof of a full, unshielded relationship with another person is the opening of the barrier that normally separates them. This barrier is erected to prevent other people seeing too closely how disordered our own inner life is in the course of everyday social intercourse while at the same time protecting us from too shattering a psychic influx emanating from emotionally unsatisfied people who would only too readily 'take over' someone else. The unprotected psyche can easily be overwhelmed by the powerful emotions of predatory individuals who are seeking, albeit unconsciously, to substantiate their own imperfect sense of identity with the strength they feel in another person.

This barrier, which is at the same time protective and

isolating, has to be breached before people can communicate with each other in depth. This depth of being is clear and unobstructed; it harbours no fear and consequently it does not flinch either from increasing self-knowledge or from the less acceptable psychic influence it may acquire from unstable people in one's vicinity. The thinning of the barrier witnesses its slow dissolution as it is irradiated and transformed by the power of the Holy Spirit within one. As I become reconciled to the depths of my being – which comprise layers of scarcely penetrable darkness as well as inextinguishable rays of sublime hope – so I can bear the depths of suffering and anguish that I sense around me in the hearts of others. Now at last, and suddenly, I discover that nothing in my fellow men, indeed in the created universe, is foreign to me. Though I myself may not have experienced the problems and difficulties that afflict those around me, I am nevertheless in such close empathy with the souls of all men in pain that I can share the psychic charge that is common to all experiences of fear, loss and dereliction. As I grow in love, so the full burden of human suffering becomes known to me. I become increasingly available to all the world's pain, which has to be borne in love before it can be transfigured by the power of the Holy Spirit.

What is the gauge of the inner depths of love? In terms of outer action love can, at least to some extent, be measured by one's capacity to sacrifice everything one holds dear in the service of the beloved. The greatest love of all is the willingness to lay down one's very life for one's friends (John 15:13). The inner revelation that energises this great sacrificial love is a spontaneous opening of the depths of the soul to the suffering of all created beings. This sudden, often dramatic, yielding of the enclosed self with its previously entrenched attitude of private interest to a total outgiving of itself to life is a divine gift. It cannot be contrived since it is outside the power of the naked will. It differs radically from the manipulated affection and feigned concern that pour out from the predatory individual who attempts to woo others for ulterior purposes. Behind this façade of affection the victim is seduced; he is subtly diminished as a responsible person and deprived of his birthright of independent action. There is a corruption of integrity and a loss of freedom which are crushed and destroyed in the chilly embrace of the predator as he implants his Judas kiss on the guileless face of his victim.

By contrast, the fullness of true love is a gift of God. It is a response of the soul to God's Spirit radiantly outpoured on the agent of healing whose demeanour in turn is warm, still, balanced and undemanding. He is at home in himself with God's gift of peace that is so very different from human comfort with its sincere, well-chosen words of reassurance. The divine peace flows out in perpetual blessing to those in communication with the person imbued with God's love. As he gives his simple, undivided attention, so those around derive from that attention an assurance of God's blessing. This radiant, childlike openness to God's renewing love can be compared to the petals of a delicate flower unfolding to confront the sun and imbibe the power of its life-giving rays. As the soul yields itself to the love of God, so it is able to give itself in full, yet unobtrusive attention to the one in need, and eventually to all who are in need. 'We for our part have crossed over from death to life; this we know, because we love our brothers' (1 John 3:14). This glorious opening of the panels of the inner life to God is a manifestation of the eternal life of His Spirit within us; the proof of its life is its bestowal of life on all who come within the orbit of its influence. As we come to know inwardly that openness from which radiates a love for an ever-increasing number of people, so we can direct our attention with greater efficacy to all those around us, and especially to the ones in pain.

'Help one another to carry these heavy loads, and in this way you will fulfil the law of Christ' (Gal. 6:2). The way of disembarrassing the other person of his load is to share it with him, not simply to take it away with magisterial authority and god-like omnipotence. The heavy load is the person's own passport to a new world in which he can be free of the entanglements of his present unsatisfactory way of life. Were he in his present disposition transparent to God's Spirit within him, he would be able himself to cope with his burden. But until he has wrestled in courage and faith with his particular incubus, he will not be worthy of the blessing of freedom, deliverance and inner transfiguration that are the fruits of God's presence in his life, of God's affirmation of his own special place in a world drawn down by torpor and sluggish unconcern for anything except its own pleasure. A new consciousness, no longer limited by what the world believes, is moulded as we bear each other's burdens in shared responsibility.

How, in fact, do we bear one another's burdens? This question sounds, at least on the surface, to be naive and simplistic. The social activist in us all would translate it in terms of relieving his distress, whether physical, economic or political. This particular approach is unexceptionable, indeed laudable, in its own context. We have already learned that the kind of religion which is without stain or fault in the sight of God our Father is this: to go to the help of orphans and widows in their distress and keep oneself untarnished by the world (Jas 1:27). But the source of all burdens is more deeply placed than this: the outer social manifestations of malaise are essentially pointers to something inherently amiss in the depth of humanity's soul. It is only too easy to concentrate one's efforts on social amelioration and reconstruction while losing sight of the unit of society, the common man, in his inner raging torment. The individual, of course, finds his justification in terms of his role in society, but until he is inwardly justified with God, his social role will remain unfulfilled and his contribution to humanity seriously diminished. Therefore the first approach to relieving another person's burdens is by an inward dedication of oneself in caring, so that the soul of the one who helps may be in union with the soul of the distraught sufferer.

To bear another person's burden is first of all to relate positively with him in the depth of silence. This again may seem strange. Surely it is more important to engage him in conversation, indeed the intense conversation of the counselling session where problems can be discussed and difficulties thrashed out in the light of unimpassioned reason? Here the dictates of common sense illuminated by psychological understanding can help mightily to disentangle the problems of life and point the way to their solution. But problems that elude direct solution by the person himself and require the assistance of a counsellor point to a significant degree of inner turmoil that is unlikely to be healed by a merely common-sense approach without some deeper contribution on the part of the counsellor, still more so of the therapist. It is when we have passed beyond the essentially rational avenues of approach and entered in faith into an unexplored way of silent unknowing that the power of the Holy Spirit is activated; He leads all those committed to God's service along an undiscovered, yet strangely familiar, path to the fulfilment of the human quest. This is an inner renewal that promises complete healing. It is at this juncture that the rational, technical modes of approach become especially helpful – they tend to fall into place quite naturally and are easily assimilated by the person in need of help.

In the deep silence of shared intent, whether there is indeed a wordless calm or merely an intense, self-revealing conversation directed in full attention to the needs of the client, there is a rapt psychic communion between the two parties. The barrier of separative individualism has been breached, so that all those involved are now veritably parts of the same body. 'Throw off falsehood; speak the truth to each other, for all of us are the parts of one body' (Eph. 4:25). The supreme falsehood on which humanity thrives until it is shriven of its illusions by the inroads of suffering and loss is the acceptance of an atomistic separation of identity of each of its members. The end of this illusion of separate identity, in which man wars against his brother and takes up arms against his own kind, is destruction and death. This is also the experience of hell: an atmosphere of total isolation of the individual from all contact with living forms as well as from a knowledge of God's all-encompassing providence.

In the converse state of heavenly consciousness there is an unobstructed flow of psychic energy from one to the other.

Nothing is withheld because there is no barrier between intimate soul communion. Heaven is artless simplicity and transparent clarity. The transparency of the true self renders it open to all other selves so that it is seen even as it sees others. The atmosphere is of God, since the Holy Spirit is both the medium of fellowship and the host at Whose table all are united in love, joy, peace and service to the world. Plotinus' vision of heaven expresses this quite marvellously,

> A pleasant life is theirs in heaven. They have the truth for mother, nurse, real being and nutriment. They see all things, not the things that are born and die, but those which have real being; and they see themselves in others. For them all things are transparent, and there is nothing dark or impenetrable, but everyone has all things in himself and sees all things in another; so that all things are everywhere, and all is all and each is all, and the glory is infinite. Each of them is great, since Yonder the small is also great. In heaven the sun is all the stars and each again and all are the sun. One thing in each is prominent above all the rest; but it also shows forth all. There pure movement reigns; for that which produces the movement, not being a stranger to it, does not trouble it. Rest is also perfect there because no principle of agitation mingles with it (*Ennead* 5, 8, 4, translated by W R Inge).

The whole object of life, at least for the human being, is to attain this state of divine coinherence, to use a word beloved by Charles Williams. And the end of the state of coinherence is its widening so as to encompass the whole created universe in its embrace. Once our souls can coinhere in the being of even one other person, we have sacrificed the assumed proprietorship of our own life and surrendered it to Someone greater than we are. And He is God. By this act of faith we have moved into the realm of eternal life under the guidance of the Holy Spirit. Heaven is not experienced in the rational consciousness of what we call normal life, which is, in fact, a travesty of true reality. The existence we tend to lead from day to day is, as we have already seen, shuttered from a full exposure to the real world, so that we may remain protected from its penetrating shafts of light and live in our own darkness. The shutter we pull down around us helps to hide our secrets from the gaze of the unfeeling world. It also excludes the unchecked psychic inflow that may issue forth from the souls of other people in pain and anguish. In both situations the shutter has a protective function as a barrier: it is a guardian against those of our unscrupulous fellows who might take advantage of our own weaknesses, and it also prevents the invasion of our personality by an overwhelming psychic surge that could severely crush us. The state of infatuation that so often masquerades as love is a cogent example of psychic projection that would tend to over- whelm and ultimately destroy the object of its attraction. In the less tangible realms of the psyche beyond mortal life there are the even more terrifying phenomena of obsession and possession by displaced discarnate entities that sometimes have a demonic power but are more often tragic lost souls in search of security and love.

We can know heaven in this life only on those rare occasions when there is complete rapport between ourselves and the other person; if there is a group of people in harmony, the experience of heaven is intensified. Now at last the shutter in front of the naked soul can be lifted and a free psychic exchange tolerated, and indeed welcomed, between all those present. In the words of Psalm 133, 'How good it is and how pleasant for brothers to live together'. The fragrance of the uninhibited mutual sharing and exchange in true worship is compared with the oil of sanctity, and its purity with the early mountain dew. 'There the Lord bestows his blessing, life for evermore.'

When we are completely open, as our souls are always open to God's scrutiny, the Spirit of God cleanses and transfigures the portals of our inner being, and we can share our most intimate thoughts with others. On an even more silent level, our responses become available to those around us, and we are, in turn, able to accept some of their scarcely tolerable burden into our own psyche. This is the work of substitution, whereby we can exchange psychic pain from a

sufferer and give him in turn the peace beyond understanding that we know as we are open to God. We are
burdened as he is relieved of his incubus. In the words of St
Paul 'For you know how generous our Lord Jesus Christ has
been: he was rich, yet for your sake he became poor, so that
through his poverty you might become rich' (2 Cor. 8:9). The
poverty of Christ is the riches of the Father, and these are
bequeathed without stint on all who cry out for help. 'Here I
stand knocking at the door; if anyone hears my voice and
opens the door, I will come in and sit down to supper with
him and he with me' (Rev. 3:20). This is also the constant cry
of divine wisdom, realised in the person of Christ. 'I am the
bread of life. Whoever comes to me shall never be hungry,
and whoever believes in me shall never be thirsty' (John
6:35). 'If anyone is thirsty let him come to me; whoever
believes in me, let him drink' (John 7:38). Wisdom cries out,
but all too seldom is the cry heeded and the divine offer
accepted. The wisdom of God finds its home within us in the
spirit of the soul; when it is tapped it yields forth an
unquenchable stream of riches, such that God alone can
bestow. There is no need any longer to seek an outside
source of authority; on the contrary, the seal of sanctity
within recognises all true spiritual authority outside itself
and responds as a brother to many other brothers. It is thus
that we respond to the authority of an authentic scripture or
spiritual tradition – it is like speaking to like, deep calling to
deep in the roar of God's cataracts, as Psalm 42 describes it.

This inner wisdom flows out to all those who are in need.
It does not simply instruct and exhort, as does worldly
wisdom; it penetrates deeply into the soul of the person in
distress and alleviates its pain by bearing its severity and
removing it. The wisdom of God is never overwhelmed by
the suffering it lays itself open to bear. It presents that
suffering to God in Christ as a transaction of exchange.
Christ, the Lamb of God Who takes away the sins of the
world, leaves peace and forgiveness in their place. The sins
Christ bears are healed by the unfailing love that accepts
them without reservation and pours out the Holy Spirit on
them. The Christian way of bearing another's burdens is

identical with the healing power of Jesus: the person is accepted for what he is, and then the Holy Spirit transforms his personality. The one thing needed of the person himself is openness to the power of love. This is the supreme act of will that all human beings are asked to make. It is the one and only willed act that ultimately matters, for man's supreme activity is the contemplation of God. It is the purpose of our life, because its end is the transformation of the person into the image of God, which is shown to us definitively in the person of Jesus Christ.

The heart of the process of bearing another's burdens is therefore to stay in silence with him and let the interchange of psychic energy take place unimpeded and uninhibited. This work of exchange is performed by the Holy Spirit, and what He requires of us is silent acquiescence. The activity of God, far from requiring any encouragement on our part, is hindered and deflected by our gratuitous interference. This applies especially when we feel impelled by a burning desire to help God actively. Until this desire loses all obsessional concern for results and all egoistical demands for praise and reassurance, it is almost certain to degenerate into officiousness and shallow worldly wisdom. In the end it may usurp God's role in its own right, so that the counsellor dominates over the Holy Spirit.

This staying in corporate silence with another person and letting the Holy Spirit perform His great work of healing the inner disorder and bestowing counsel on the cleansed soul is at once the simplest activity and the most profound. Of the counsellor it demands such a transparent self-knowledge that no element from the unconscious can be expected to obtrude and obscure the radiance of God's Spirit within him. Obviously such an invasion of unconscious material into the field of consciousness can never be prevented by an act of will. Its baneful effect is obviated by the power of love radiating so strongly and insistently from within us that it can intercept, greet and enfold all that is unclean or perverse, whether it comes from our own darkness or from the darkness of the collective unconscious, from which we inherit the psychic information as well as the destructive tendencies that have arisen from creature activity since life started. Christ did not flinch from any human experience, nor turn his back on any who were in need, no matter how sordid their way of life or degraded their circumstances. He was open in direct awareness to the full gamut of human experience. This is very different from viewing the degraded and diseased at a distance, from the vantage-point of self-imposed domination where one can look down in judgmental pity and dispense the medicine of worldly wisdom in lordly condescension. In a truly healing relationship the medicine of God's power has first to cleanse one's own soul of its separativeness and subversion. Only then can that medicine of grace act through one to heal the other person. And furthermore, the cleansed soul is now an integral part of the divine balm that restores the health of that which was diseased and perverted. Thus the true counsellor is not only the channel of the Holy Spirit; he is also the refined instrument of that Spirit. He is used as an aid in healing by the Holy Spirit; he does not impress himself on others as a healing agent, but is used in his humility as the representative of Christ to effect the cure. We do God's work best when we offer ourselves to Him in steadfast love, saying 'Thy will be done', and then becoming servants in stillness. That stillness is perfected by God to become a peace that brings all created forms into a vortex of transforming love in which a new being is fashioned.

In this state of self-renunciation, the Holy Spirit issues forth from the counsellor, who now becomes a radiant instrument of God's healing power; it is, indeed, at this point that the ministries of healing and counselling merge to become one great service of reconciliation and trans-figuration. The darkness of the one in need is taken in exchange by the minister of God's grace; in Him it is lightened and healed. In turn, the Holy Spirit descends into, or more correctly issues effectively from the soul of the one who has been disembarrassed of his heavy incubus of darkness and despair. The Spirit can now lead the person into a full confrontation of his problem and show him the way to its solution. This seldom involves a miraculous release. Much more often it consists of a patient coping with the difficulty, but now with the conscious support of God. In due course the journey comes to its end and the person emerges much stronger in character as a result of the ordeal. Thus a blessing has been obtained by the power of the Holy Spirit working through the love and dedication of the counsellor.

This ministry of silence in deep fellowship with the afflicted may seem vague, insubstantial and visionary to the rationalist and sceptic who feels that extravert activity is the key to true relationships at all levels. But until we have experienced the inner release of tension and anxiety that tranquillity brings, we shall never know the healing power of God in silence. In silence we can not only hear the articulated cry of the one in need, but can also sense it on a far more interior psychic level. If we know the power of love as an inner reality we can rest assured that we are worthy of exchanging the quota of suffering with the other person. And then healing commences. As the man born blind said of Jesus' healing power, 'All I know is this: once I was blind, now I can see' (John 9:25). The divine exchange of Jesus' love and the Spirit that illuminated it heralded the healing, and its fruit was the birth of a resolute man enabled to grow into spiritual maturity.

6.

The Way of Unknowing

The way of counsel, that counsel which enlivens the heart and renews the soul, is the way of God's grace to us. Those who are His chosen instruments to spread His word and bring life to the spiritually dead, are themselves, at least in that moment of divine transference, dead to both the world's wisdom and their own deep awareness of inadequacy in the face of the ultimate mystery. The mark of true sanctity is a humility focused on a constant awareness of inadequacy. The closer one is to God in spirit, the more conscious one is of one's stain. This stain is a lack of love. It is not a morbid introspective analysis of past misdemeanours; it is an acknowledgment of the shutter between oneself and the reality of love which is a sharing of self in service to the world. When we have acknowledged our persistent inadequacy – and even the seraphs could not bear to face God directly in Isaiah's great vision in the temple, as they called ceaselessly to one another the words of the Sanctus – God removes that shutter from our souls by His act of eternal forgiveness, and at last we can say, with Isaiah, 'Here am I; send me' (Isa. 6:1–8). Then we are completely open to God's Spirit and can proclaim His word, the word proclaimed in Scripture and interpreted by the Spirit to bring wisdom to the age in which we live and to the people we serve.

When we are dead to the world's wisdom we enter the cloud of unknowing. In the words of the spiritual classic of that name 'For when I say darkness, I mean a lack of knowing: as all thing that thou knowest not, or hast forgotten, is dark to thee; for thou seest it not with thy ghostly eye. And for this reason it is called, not a cloud of the air, but a *cloud of unknowing*; which is betwixt thee and thy God' (chap. 4). The text goes on to tell us that we have also to forget our own past and present distractions if we are to come to God. 'And if ever thou shalt come to this cloud and will dwell and work therein as I bid thee, thou must, as this *cloud of unknowing* is above thee, betwixt thee and thy God, right so put a *cloud of forgetting* beneath thee, betwixt thee and all the creatures that ever he made' (chap. 5). This is the supreme act of faith; it is the equivalent in the realm of intellectual speculation and worldly progress of following Jesus' command to give up one's life for His sake and the Gospel. The prize is the knowledge and attainment of eternal life, which is the life of the Spirit within the soul of each one of us. But it is discovered only in making the act of faith in renunciation of all that is apparently secure in order to give of oneself fully in love to God Whom one dimly knows and one's fellow men whom one believes one knows only too well.

The glorious sequel to this act of faith is that nothing God had previously given us is taken away; instead, it is confirmed and transfigured by a radiance that finds its source in the Holy Spirit. He is eternally renewing all things until that far-off, yet ever-heralded event which will witness the spiritualisation of the whole universe. The spirit of counsel reveals itself to us when we bid farewell to all preconceptions and have, by a positive act of trust, yielded ourselves naked and unprotected by any intellectual subterfuge to God.

This giving of ourself unconditionally to God entails first a frank acknowledgment of our present inadequacy that shows itself in our recurrently sinful attitude to life – in which the shutter is pulled down to shield the soul from a full exposure to and participation in the lives of our fellow men. This is the conscious confession that we make to ourselves in alert awareness in the presence of God. It is the precondition for the subsequent joyous release that follows God's unconditional forgiveness. To ask in willed intent in prayer is to receive God's love, and the proof of that love is the opening up of a new perspective of reality in which all are one, and the One Who is perfect embraces all. Now we are enfolded in the cloud of forgetting, and our gaze is directed to that One alone Who can grant us salvation and give us enlightenment, the Spirit of God. He is both our mentor and the destination of our journey into wisdom.

This is the supreme act of contemplation: the naked, unobscured soul faces the radiant effulgence of God's presence. It is filled with awe that at once is transformed and expanded into rapturous love. No one can face God directly and remain alive; this is true of ego-consciousness. But when the ego is sacrificed, and the personality is pierced in love on behalf of even one other creature, the spirit of the soul can focus so directly on to the divine presence that the person of God becomes immediately available to the one who has sacrificed himself. The Spirit of God is now fully alive in the person's consciousness, and the wisdom of God unfolds its counsel in his soul. The Spirit illumines every aspect of the personality: the soul is cleansed and purified, the rational mind enlightened, the emotions purged of selfish desires and enriched by the influx of love for all creatures, and the body made new and vibrant with living power. This is the heart of the healing process; it is nothing less than a re-creation of the human person in the divine image. When one is filled with the effulgent splendour of God, one enters more completely into the knowledge and life of God. 'And because for us there is no veil over the face, we all reflect as in a mirror the splendour of the Lord; thus we are transfigured into His likeness from splendour to splendour; such is the influence of the Lord who is Spirit' (2 Cor. 3:18).

The power from on high does not invade the personality, still less dismember or destroy it in order to replace it with something different. Instead it respects and makes full use of every gift, every experience that has contributed to the present stature of the person, and everything that has been learned through diligent study and painstaking observation. The end is that the treasury of individual endeavour may be transformed from a mere witness of past experience to an instrument of immediate usefulness for the work ahead of it. When we are able to let go of the emotional echoes of what has already passed away and relinquish the agonised charge of longing and remorse for that which is no longer within the grasp of our recall, we are filled with the warm after-glow of the experience behind us. What was summed up in the past has been realised in our growth up to the present, and now its riches are available to us for our work in the future. And at last we are able to confront a fellow human being in clarity of vision and attentiveness of soul so that we may see his burden and share his pain with an authority of inner direction that proceeds from God Himself.

God alone knows the ultimate answer to every human question for He sees each creature in its final completion, an end of growth contributed to equally by divine grace and the patient development of the will of the person struggling towards integrity of purpose and fulfilment of design. God's love to us is shown in His respect for our own individuality. God loves us so much that He does not withhold suffering from us. Rather than reduce us to the impotence of docile puppets who follow slavishly after the dictatorial will of their master, He has made us masters of our fate by endowing us with a centre of direction within the depth of the personality. This centre is the soul, and its free action is the will. The divine spark is the spirit of the soul; when we know this point as a living experience, we know God and the Word eternally begotten from Him, even Christ the Lord. This Word now directs and empowers the will, so that God's will and man's will work together in an integrated personality for the work of healing and integrating other people individually, society collectively and all creation universally.

The work of spiritual counselling is to set the client free of past psychological encumbrances so that the Holy Spirit can penetrate into his soul as a cleansing fire and a directing light. The soul can then act according to its own wisdom and the will can at last be authentically free. In God's service there is alone perfect freedom, because in doing His work the agent is liberated from the impediments that mar his own personality – the fear of past inadequacy recalled as a remorseless incubus to present action, the desire for approval by one's peers which is a way of averting one's gaze once more from one's own inadequacy by basking in the appreciation of other people, and the resentment that stems from failing to attain what one believes is one's due reward. In the way of unknowing the minister of counsel implants the word of God deeply into the soul of the one who cries out in pain. This he does through silent compassion in shared fellowship.

God's strength is always made perfect in human weakness, because when we feel bereft of any effectual encouragement or counsel, we open ourselves spontaneously to the Holy Spirit. It is, as it were, that we are calling, albeit unconsciously, on the name of the Lord in the agony of our darkness, which is shared by the one who comes to us for help. In the cloud of unknowing the still small voice of God, Who is spirit, comes to us and flows through us to the deepest, holiest part of the other person's psyche. This is the spirit of the soul, and once it is activated its own store of treasured wisdom is released and made available to the one in need. The ministry of contemplation, though focused on God, soon extends into the personality of the one in need of counsel and therapy. It not only shares the burden of his distress and substitutes its own robust strength for the vague paralysing fears that cripple him and render him impotent, but it also directs the Spirit of God deep into his naked, unshuttered soul and sets in action the work of the Holy Spirit within him. In this respect the Holy Spirit is both the universal power from on high that spiritualises all matter and raises it through death to immortality, and the focus of light that burns constantly in the spirit of man leading him to fresh endeavours that find their end in death and resurrection. That which is beyond our comprehension is nearer to us than the knowledge of our own identity. God, who is often very distant from the imagination of the intellectually proficient and scientifically erudite, is the eternal host of the small child. Indeed, we have to become once more as little children if we are to enter the Kingdom of

God, for it is available only to those who have the unshuttered openness of vision of an innocent child (Mark 10:15).

Why then should we grow up to adult stature and participate wholeheartedly in the grimy commerce of worldly strife? We soon lose the glow of pristine innocence and adolescent idealism as our personalities become tarnished with the stain of the world's unrighteousness. St Paul says 'When I was a child, my speech, my outlook and my thoughts were all childish. When I grew up, I had finished with childish things. Now we see only puzzling reflections in a mirror, but then we shall see face to face' (1 Cor. 13:10–12). Acquiring the knowledge of worldly things gives us a closer empathy with our fellow men. The burden of possessions and the incubus of family responsibility bring us into closer relationship on a workaday level with our brethren who are similarly encumbered. The gaining of a reputation for skill in a particular occupation or profession makes us more sensitive to the demands of society that we should serve our fellow creatures with integrity and self-giving devotion. In this way the rather individualistic private life that we enjoyed as a child – assuming always that we were supported with the love of caring parents in a wholesome family unit, an assumption that becomes more problematic as family loyalty disintegrates and personal moral discipline declines – has now to be broadened and extended to include many other types of people until nothing in the world is foreign to us.

Furthermore, the wisdom of God that is an innate gift of the soul, has to penetrate and transform the whole person so that he too may assume a god-like role in the world – by this I mean one of collaborating actively in willed assent with the creative power of the Most High. The expertise of man that shows itself in the amazing scientific and technological advances of our modern age is the way in which God has imbued us with His Spirit, so that we may understand the mechanism of creation more dynamically and aid in the eternal work of renewal of the world. But until the creative potential of the human mind is redeemed from the bondage of selfish striving and predatory desire for total hegemony, man's efforts are consummated in an orgy of destruction. It is doubtful whether people are any more depraved now than in previous ages; on the contrary, there seems to be a steady increase in international concern for the conservation of resources and social justice embracing all the world's population irrespective of race or creed. But unfortunately this acknowledgement of the oneness of all life is too slow in comparison with the tumultuous advance of technological knowledge and scientific understanding that has characterised the modern world.

We are today rather like power-intoxicated adolescents, but a return to innocent childhood is both impossible and undesirable. What is needed is a full growth into mature adult stature in which the vast scientific power at our disposal can be used responsibly and with compassion for the needs of all creation. This is achieved by being constantly open in love to God in acknowledged ignorance and to our brethren in self-transcending devotion. The way is one of contemplative prayer; the end is a fertilisation of the power-weary personality by the fragrant balm of the Holy Spirit Who both renews us personally and shows us the way of beneficent employment of the scientific resources at our disposal, a gift that is bestowed on us by the power of that Spirit. In this way the wisdom of man, also a gift of God's Spirit, is led into new fields of exploration and endeavour by a participation in the foolishness of God, which alone simplifies the abstruse and makes wise the simple.

The innocent child we are to become in order to accept God's kingdom is therefore not the self-centred baby we once were. It is the simplicity of the adult shriven of all conceit and selfishness by the slow attrition of experience, suffering and fellowship, so that he is at last open to and aware of the one thing needful for salvation: the presence of God Who is closer to him than his awareness of his own identity. The person young in spiritual knowledge clings to and relies on the intellectual opinions of the present age as his arbiter of wisdom and authority. The more experienced soul opens itself to God in joyous unknowing and self-forgetting. In the words of the Magnificat 'The hungry he has filled with good things, the rich sent empty away' (Luke 1:53). The good thing that comes to us by the way of unknowing is the inspiration of the Holy Spirit Who leads us into a more comprehensive understanding of the truth. This He does not only by a fresh revelation but also by enabling us to use the knowledge we already possess to greater advantage. When the ego is put in its right place, the Spirit of God can make all wisdom available to us. Not a little of that wisdom is already ours by virtue of what we have read, even in the distant past of our childhood and youth, and have subsequently relegated to the backrooms of our mind. These apparently forgotten fragments of our memory can be recalled in an emergency when we are still and open to God's Spirit within us. But now they cease to be mere pieces of disconnected information and are instead welded into a coherent whole, the wisdom of the ages concentrated into a single moment of time, by the power of the Holy Spirit. At the same time a new perspective is given us so that the well-worn teachings of Scripture are suddenly invested with a contemporary meaning. All genuinely spiritual teaching is on this account of timeless value, because it speaks from the depth of human experience and issues forth from the soul of the one who is inspired to the end that all who listen may be changed into real people. Its truth is not dependent on the cultural background of the teacher, but speaks universally to all people of all ages according to their willingness and ability to receive and assimilate the message. Thus the young Jesus spoke with a unique authority that at once arrested and transformed the common people who heard Him. Today His words have a similarly transforming effect, but only to those who have been jolted out of their customary indolence and complacency, usually by some life-shattering event. The person who comes for counsel is often in that situation, and the one whose privilege it is to lead him into a fresh appreciation of truth must be the agent of the Holy Spirit and not merely the purveyor of worldly wisdom. The wisdom of the worldly ones tends merely towards a more contemporary version of the status quo. The wisdom of

God, tapped in the way of unknowing, acts as a catalyst and evokes a new and entirely heightened response so that a changed person emerges from the encounter with truth.

Our own life story is in the end our manual of discipline as well as our book of wisdom. It is our unique gift to all who meet us, and it is, at least when we die, our presentation of ourselves to God as part of the judgment, however we attempt to visualise it, that follows our death and resurrection in a new form. We do not need to provide others with an autobiographical account of our own lives and struggles, so as to compare them with those of the ones whom we are trying to help. Indeed, it is unwise to compare oneself with anyone else, at least in his presence, even when the desire is to encourage him on the way. Although we may have much in common with certain types of people, the personal flavour is always distinctive in its uniqueness. On the other hand, the Holy Spirit uses our past experiences and the wisdom that has accrued from their patient assimilation to guide and encourage all who approach us for help. The Spirit puts the right words in our mind apposite to the immediate situation, so that a point of contact between an aspect of our past life and that of the person seeking counsel is made apparent. It is far better not to discuss one's own past with the one needing counsel, but rather to let that past speak for itself through the personality that presents itself to the world in general and to the client in particular. What I am as a person shouts out to anyone with sensitivity by the psychic currents that emanate from me. These are much more revealing pointers to my authentic nature than either my mental prowess or my professional qualifications. It is the psychic currents that link, or repel, the souls of others and mine. If I am repulsive to the other person, no amount of technical knowledge will be of any avail. If I can effect psychic rapport, healing will flow out to the one in need even if my academic knowledge of psychology is limited. The best result occurs, of course, when psychic sensitivity is aligned to specialised psychological knowledge. This is not, in my experience, a very usual concurrence, since psychological erudition tends to separate the practitioner from the one needing help by making him feel superior and act in an officious way. But when the counsellor has already traversed his own hell, he may then attain the priceless ability of relating psychically as well as intellectually with his client. At this point the spirit of counsel becomes the spirit of healing also.

The way of unknowing is the way also of humility. It sees the ongoing process of life as an adventure to be experienced and enjoyed rather than a foregone conclusion merely to be confirmed. The humble of the world are able to receive the joy of the present moment with a childlike wonder that never grows stale with familiarity. When all preconceptions are separated from one's field of response by the cloud of unknowing and all personal prejudice divested from one by the cloud of forgetting, one enters a completely changed understanding of life. One can greet each fresh event with enthusiasm, for every new thing that confronts one is also a means to one's liberation from the narrow confines of the world's vision. What is unknown but followed in faith leads us to an experience of God's unending providence. St Paul speaks of 'things beyond our seeing, things beyond our hearing, things beyond our imagining, all prepared by God for those who love Him' (1 Cor. 2:9). To love God means to be open to His grace in silent contemplation. The fruit of that contemplation is the ability to bring down love to the world. Its proof in action is the capacity to bear another person's burden as a preliminary to making him responsive to the Holy Spirit Who is both our leader into truth and the One who fills us with holy counsel. By the way of unknowing one can enter into a life-transcending relationship with an ever-growing number of people until the mystical unity of all life in God is revealed in its splendour.

7.

Psychic Communion and Counselling

There are three ways in which we can experience communication: physical, psychical and spiritual. In physical communication there is sensory stimulation that can be responded to directly by the rational mind through the agency of the brain. In psychical communication there is an apparently direct contact from the deepest layer of consciousness of one person to another; it is from soul to soul. It is extrasensory inasmuch as it bypasses the organs of sensation and perception and yet impinges itself directly on the mind where it is accepted, acknowledged and made the object of response according to one's rational powers. In the psychic mode one person may be apprised of someone else's inner disposition without previous knowledge of his background or his private life. It was said of Jesus that He knew men so well, all of them, that He needed no evidence from others about a man, for He Himself could tell what was in a man (John 2:25). This is psychical attunement at its most immaculate.

Since the soul is not limited by the time sequence and will, we believe, continue to progress in spiritual knowledge and grow in stature even after the death of the physical body, psychic information can impinge on future events and tap into the past also. The well-attested phenomena of precognition and retrocognition provide compelling illustrations of the relative nature of time in the psychic mode. Soul can communicate directly with soul, in this world and apparently also in the life beyond death, however inadequately we may picture it from our own point of vantage. It is not uncommon for recently bereaved people to have what is for them an incontrovertible experience of direct psychic contact from a loved one, the result being an inner conviction that all is well with the deceased and that the bond of love remains intact. These impressions are necessarily fleeting and nebulous in quality so that they cannot be imparted with authority to other people, especially those who are compulsively sceptical. It is noteworthy that when Jesus arose from the dead He appeared only to those who had loved Him, however inadequately. It was only after He had ascended into the Kingdom of God that He enjoyed mystical unity with the Father, and then He could appear in His spiritual radiance to an infinitely wider range of people, including those who had been previously hostile, like St Paul.

The most exalted type of communication is indeed the spiritual in which there is a direct flow of love and wisdom from God to man. In its most profound and glorious form, mystical illumination, the barrier that separates the uncreated radiance of God from the dark torpor of the human mind is momentarily lifted, and the person can gain a direct insight into divine reality that is of life-transforming urgency. But there are also less intense experiences in which the timid soul is lifted momentarily up out of its customary gloom and apathy and brought into a concentrated focus of radiant light and encompassing love, so that a more emphatic purpose guides its hesitant steps once more. The spiritual mode of communication, however humble it may appear to be, has the effect of raising the person to whom it reveals itself from a narrowly selfish vision of life to one that is self-transcending and sees as its end the service and healing of humanity, indeed of all created beings. Like the psychic mode of communication, it is extrasensory and it impinges itself directly on the soul of the person to whom it comes as a gift of grace.

Spiritual communication is always beneficial, but psychical and physical types of contact vary in their quality according to the source of the information. Psychic communication, for instance, can be of evil import and life-destroying potency if it emanates from a demonic source, which may be either a depraved human being or a perverted entity in the life beyond death. This is why indiscriminate trafficking with psychical forces is strongly deprecated in the world's higher religious teachings. Unwise types of meditation techniques can also open a sensitive person to psychic invasion from outside as well as from the untapped depths of his own unconscious psyche.

The end of the spiritual life is the spiritualisation of all things. This means the raising and transforming of both the physical and the psychical dimensions of reality from egoistical domination to full communion with God. In this respect we see the presage of this spiritualisation in God's Word Who became flesh and dwelt among us and Whose immaculate psychic sensitivity is the end to which our communion with those around us leads. It must be emphasised that we are meant to communicate physically and psychically while we live on earth, for without a vigorous body and a sensitive soul we could not actualise ourselves fully as people. We relate to all forms of creation physically and psychically, while the wisdom of God reaches us spiritually and is interpreted by the mind to form the basis of worldly understanding, scientific knowledge and social enlightenment. It is also received into the soul as love which emanates psychically to all around it, so that God's eternal blessing may be imparted freely to all living forms throughout the world.

This, I believe, is the basis of what is called spiritual healing, and it forms the foundation of effective counselling. The minister of healing is one who can attain a strong rapport, even an intimate relationship of caring, with the person whom he is serving. And in that self-giving which is the measure of all effective relationships, the power of the Holy Spirit flows from the one who serves to the one who is in need, and healing of the whole person is initiated. This is not merely a bodily healing or even a mental or emotional restoration; it is a total re-creation of the individual into something of the measure of a complete person. A person, in this respect, is a fully functioning human being working from a centre of independent judgment and decision through the agency of a freed, active will. In other words, there is an integration of the personality around the central focus of the spirit that illuminates the soul. This in turn transmits a more enduring meaning for existence to the rational mind and the emotions than a mere desire for immediate survival and the satisfaction of the body's needs that dominate the perspective of the unrealised man. The work of healing and counselling, in their different ways, is that of sending the power of God's Spirit to the person in need, and this transmission is effected psychically. It follows therefore that the more lucid and unobstructed the psyche of the one who ministers, the more effective will be his work and the greater will be the benefit he bestows on those he serves. Furthermore, he will be less liable to fatigue and psychic depletion in his arduous work, as he is able to call in prayer on the Holy Spirit at all times, especially when he knows he is in special need of protection.

We give apparently of ourselves, but in fact what comes through us is the Word and Spirit of God. As we give God's power to those in need, so we are replenished for the work of healing, and eventually we add our quota of life to the Spirit of God in our service to those around us. If we try to give everything on our own, unaided, without deference to God and calling upon Him ceaselessly in prayer, we insidiously elevate ourselves, at least in our own estimation, to god-like status. The result is severe bodily strain and psychic depletion which will soon render any further healing work impossible. The way of exchange and substitution that we have already seen as the heart of an authentic healing relationship, in which the burdens of one person are borne by another, is psychic communion at its most spiritually vibrant. The love and devotion that mark such empathy lift the burden to God Who transforms it into a blessing for the person who had borne it for so long and also for the one who had served him in the capacity of counsellor. As soon as we offer our souls and bodies as a sacrifice for other people in the name of God – and this means in loving devotion – He is with us and the Spirit encompasses us in the deepest psychic communion. We in turn give that Spirit to all whom we serve in love, so that integration may commence in the lives of many people.

In my own experience in the ministry of healing and counselling I have been impressed by the quality of blessing that can come through the silence of compassion. When one has been rendered speechless in the face of a terrible human tragedy, the Holy Spirit can implant the word of intimate encouragement directly into the soul of the one who suffers during the silence of unknowing. On one such occasion I was asked to pay a hospital visit to a man whom I had never previously met shortly after he had undergone a very extensive operation for cancer. He was not at all pleased to see me though he had been apprised of my proposed visit shortly before the operation, and had then signified his wish that I should come to see him. He felt thoroughly miserable because he was in great discomfort, and could not face having to participate in the spiritually edifying conversation which he expected me to initiate. I was impelled – without premeditation – simply to sit still in a chair next to his bed and tell him to be quiet with me. The silence lasted about five minutes; when we emerged from it his appearance was completely different. A glow of warmth played about his face and his eyes were vibrant with life. He was speechless with amazed delight, and so was I. God had used me, through being completely receptive and self-effacing, as His instrument of peace to that man, and now the Holy Spirit was working actively in him as a healing power. Indeed, his recovery was remarkably rapid and uneventful considering the gravity of his malady, and he later entered the healing ministry himself. 'My grace is all you need; power comes to its full strength in weakness' (2 Cor. 12:9).

This, of course, does not belittle the work that must be done on the physical and mental level in the full ministries of healing and counselling. It simply puts them into their proper perspective. As Jesus says: 'Set your mind on God's kingdom and His justice before everything else, and all the rest will come to you as well' (Matt. 6:33). Once our spiritual relationship to God is aligned with our psychical relation-ship to our fellow men, His Spirit will inform all our efforts, whether physical, mental or emotional, made on behalf of those who seek our help.

It must also be said that there are people of considerable psychic sensitivity who do not have any belief in a power of transcendent might and love whom men call God. This, in itself, may not pose an insuperable barrier to spiritual understanding, especially when we consider the cruelty that man has often visited on his neighbour in the name of the God he so confidently worships. But the ultimate criterion of spirituality is one's attitude to the world and to one's fellow man, as summed up in the two great commandments of Jesus: the love of God with all one's being and the love of one's neighbour as oneself. To some, notably those of an innately mystical disposition, the love of the unseen God comes as the primary revelation. To others, especially the more extravert type of individual, it is deep personal relationships, at first enclosed and rather limited, that eventually open their eyes to the being and love of God. In fact, only when we love God in mystical devotion can we love our neighbour perfectly also, because personal love devoid of the consciously divine base tends to become demanding and possessive. When we love the whole created universe and the One Who fashioned all things, we shall not confuse the creature with the Creator, and we shall also see our own priorities in their proper perspective. All personal relationships wither with the passage of time, but when they are consummated in commitment to God they assume something of the nature of immortality.

To put these reflections on a more practical level, one may consider the person who possesses as an innate quality a strong psychic sensitivity and power. He may be able to make deep relationships with people and effect an impressive amount of healing work. But the temptation to use this gift to gain power over others will be enormous, just as will the tendency to regard himself as superior to others and to use them for his own selfish purposes. The history of occultism emphasises this destructive tendency among those who use native psychic gifts on a basically personal level, seeing themselves as the arbiters of their right or wrong usage. This was the primal sin of Adam and Eve who took on themselves the power of judging between good and evil without divine grace. Whenever a person assumes a god-like role without the prior sanction of God Himself, he takes on the quality of Antichrist, and whatever he does, especially when he believes he has the world's best interests at heart, becomes aberrant and demonic. On the other hand, when a god-like role is bestowed on a person by the Deity as part of his minor work in the world, and for a short period of time only, that person becomes transparent in goodness, fully open in love to all created things, and of a radiant spiritual beauty. He is, in other words, Christ-like, and his end is self-sacrifice, not self-aggrandisement. His radiance is so transparent that anyone who is sensitive to spiritual truth can sense the soul within him – I would indeed go so far as to say the soul is visible according to the harmlessness and love of the person who manifests it in the world. Thus it can be said of Jesus that the Father and He are one (John 10:30). By contrast, the souls of many of us are so encrusted in the debris of assertive sensual existence which is an accretion of wrong bodily usage, that their light is largely obscured in everyday life. Impending death or a terrible disaster often serves to restore that light, to some extent at least, for the person's great journey into the unseen world beyond his grasp. But by then most of his life may have been lamentably misspent.

It follows that many, if not all, the gifts of the Spirit enumerated by St Paul in 1 Corinthians 12 are mediated psychically, though they all should come directly from God as a spiritual endowment. We read in Matthew 7:21–23 the following important statement:

Not everyone who calls me 'Lord, Lord' will enter the kingdom of Heaven, but only those who do the will of my heavenly Father. When that day comes, many will say to me 'Lord, Lord did we not prophesy in your name, cast out devils in your name, and in your name perform many miracles?' Then I will tell them to their face, 'I never knew you; out of my sight, you and your wicked ways!'.

It is evident from this saying that unspiritual people may exhibit gifts of the Holy Spirit, using these gifts on an unacceptable basis of personal advancement, even in the name of Christ. In the end it must be that all gifts come from the Holy Spirit, inasmuch as God is in charge of all things. His sun rises on good and bad alike, and He sends the rain on the honest and dishonest (Matt. 5:45). But if the gift is to be fully spiritualised, it must be given back to God in thanksgiving and humility. At this point the workings of the Holy Spirit in the life of the person cease to be merely an unconscious force – since the Holy Spirit's first action in our world is that of Lord and giver of life – and become the conscious light of the fully awakened person that leads him to an expanded understanding of God's plan in his life. In other words, the Holy Spirit takes His undisputed place as sovereign of our individual conscience, which was previously dominated by our conditioning and the demands of our peers with whom we work day by day. When the Holy Spirit acts within us as a consciously acknowledged power, the God of love is our sole source of devotion, and that devotion pours forth in unfailing love to all our neighbours. We are now hidden in that love, and our one aim is to give it as perfectly as we can to those in need.

In this state of selfless devotion, our innate psychic sensitivity will be quickened; even those who deny any such awareness will discover that they seem to know the inner disposition of the person they are counselling. They will appear to be given direct information about their client's needs, and what they say will be uncanny in its pertinence. This is not to be interpreted as an intrusive prying into the inner life of another individual, a meddling in his private affairs. The insight comes as a shaft of enlightenment, for the Holy Spirit is directing all our endeavours towards a confrontation with the soul of the one who is in need of healing or counsel. As the truth is shown and shared spontaneously and in good faith, so a feeling of release is experienced by both the counsellor and the client. The remarkable feature of authentic psychic communion is that both parties are led into the truth of a situation, so that the barriers of the past are lifted and the light of understanding bathes the personalities, cleansing them of diffidence, fear and mistrust. In other words, a true psychic communion strengthens the counsellor no less than the one who seeks counsel. In a real therapeutic relationship the healing is eventually visited on all who have taken part in the transaction. As we give, so we are given to the end that all may partake more fully of God's healing spirit. When the counsellor has been enabled to effect psychic contact and give the word of release to the person he is assisting, he will in all probability tend to forget the message he imparted. Once this has done its work of healing it remains a treasured possession of the person to whom it was delivered. It is no longer relevant to the work of the counsellor. Indeed, he must now move on to the next task revealed by the Holy Spirit and not spend valuable time reflecting on past work successfully completed.

The way of deeper communion with the soul of another person is also the journey to a more profound knowledge of oneself. If I am in direct communication with my inner being, I shall be open to all relevant psychic impressions coming from those around me. Far from having to strive to attain this knowledge, I have merely to be quiet and relaxed. Openness to God renders me available to minister to the needs of all those who need me – and indeed by the power of prayer to a vast, unseen concourse separated by space and time but united by the eternal love that God bestows on all His creatures. Transparency to the depth of one's own psyche brings an openness to the psychic emanations of those who seek one's help. Whether this assistance is of the unpremeditated substitutionary kind that bears another's emotional burdens or of a consciously directive type that imparts new information to that person depends on the will of God. While counselling is best if it tends towards a non-directive approach, so that the person in need can be assisted to make his own decisions once he is released from destructive tension and emotional turmoil – a therapeutic effect of a fine counselling session – it is nevertheless often the case that the interview impels him towards a changed perspective and a more positive approach to his problems. This will culminate in a consciously applied decision that is bound to influence the future course of his life.

Another fascinating psychic phenomenon that not infrequently shows itself in the practice of those who are well attuned to their fellows in their work of loving service is a startling tendency for apparently unrelated events to throw a powerful light on the problem immediately confronting them. It may be the unheralded emergence of a topic in a casual conversation that suddenly highlights a factor previously overlooked, or else a sentence from a book which one has been spontaneously compelled by an inner impulse to open and read that brings a fresh insight to the circumstance that is occupying one's present attention. Indeed, as St Paul saw so clearly, 'All things work together for good for those who love God' (Rom. 8:28). The Holy Spirit co-operates for good with those who dedicate themselves to God's service, having been called according to His purpose. This is, I believe, an aspect of the meaningful coincidence of contingent, or chance, events termed 'synchronicity' by Carl Jung, and which he discovered during his psychotherapeutic studies with people who were steadily attaining individuation following a progressive integration of the previously fragmented parts of their personality. Jung stressed the acausal nature of the concurrence of these events: that the one did not precipitate or influence the other, but that each seemed to be a sign or manifestation of an underlying psychic accord that binds together in unity all apparently disconnected events. This unity shows itself in the cosmic harmony that is known to the mystic in his moment of illumination, and is, when all life has been consummated to God by the willed intent of His creatures, to become universally manifest as a realm of expanded, coherent thought and enlightened action.

On a more immediately practical level it seems that, as we become more fully integrated as people, so our inner relationships with others become stabilised, extended and exalted. The power of healing, which is our innate psychic emanation now purified by the Holy Spirit working freely and without distortion within us, flows out to those people in our close vicinity and also affects the life of the less developed creatures around us. These include not only our animal relatives but also the vegetation with which we share a common existence in this world of potentially abundant life. Even what appear to be the inanimate forces and forms of nature are not beyond the range of psychic influence emanating from a truly enlightened, saintly individual. As one grows in psychic sensitivity, so one's solidarity with all life and all created forms becomes more perfectly realised. This solidarity is no mere sentimental effusion or intellectual abstraction; it is an outpouring of blessing on to the entire world around one. This blessing is effected by a conscious concern that finds its end in constructive action, and also by an uncontrived, essentially unconscious attitude of harm-lessness and tranquillity.

When we are at peace within the depths of our own being, we are placed in alignment with the psychic power of life that is the gift of the Holy Spirit. The inner peace that we know becomes at last a peace that is shared with those near us and finally also with those who are far away. This sharing is a function of intercessory prayer that is a product of the practice of contemplation. Once we can face God directly in love and thanksgiving, we are deemed worthy of a place between Him and His creatures, and through us flows the restored psychic power that is bestowed by the Holy Spirit as part of God's spiritual radiance. Prayer plays an essential part in our attainment of inner psychic balance; it is also the means by which we impart equilibrium to the world in faith and peace. When we can begin to see the work of counselling and healing in this inspiring light, we can glimpse the extent and glory of the influence of the Holy Spirit as the sanctifying power of God in the lives of all His creatures.

The peace that passes understanding has in the end to flow from each of us acting as God's chosen vessel. Only when we are spiritually awake and in conscious communion with God can we be in psychic communion with those around us. The power of the Holy Spirit will bring all living forms into harmonious interaction so that healing can proceed on a universal scale. This is the full vision of the spirit of counsel, that the love and wisdom of God should bring together all apparently separate elements into a fully functioning body, alive with hope and vibrant with eager expectation, led by a restored, resolute humanity.

8.

The Discernment of Spirits

The spirit of counsel is a gift of the Holy Spirit that enables
us to discern motives and their sources, to distinguish that
which is authentically of God from that which issues from a
source that is psychically based but assumes a divine
authority. All life is communication, and the final
assessment of the value of any one life is the depth of
relationship it has effected with as many other living forms
as have been in its reach of attainment. As Martin Buber
says, 'All real living is meeting'. When the judgment comes
after our death, we shall be tested not on what we have
attained in terms of possessions, knowledge or power in this
world, but on the depth of relationship we have attained
with our fellow men. As St John of the Cross puts it: 'When
the evening comes, we will be judged on love'. We shall have
more to reflect on this sombre, yet strangely liberating
theme later.

The spirit of discernment helps us to discern the spirits.
We remember St John's warning (1 John 4:1–2), not to trust
any and every spirit, but to test them all to see whether they
are of God. The Spirit of God acknowledges that Jesus
Christ has come in the flesh, an acknowledgment that is
something more than a mere theological affirmation. It is an
undertaking that we shall follow the way that He showed
when He lived among us, to the end that we may attain
mature humanity measured by nothing less than His full
stature (Eph. 4:13). This spirit of discernment is also the
spirit of discipline, the true way of the disciple, that we have
to obey if the spirit of counsel is to do its work effectively
through us. Only then can we be an immaculate instrument

for the healing work entrusted to us by God.

It would seem from what we have already noted that the way of effective counselling is traversed more by patient, trustful silence than by assertive action and masterful interference and direction. Since the true Counsellor is always the Holy Spirit, it is not to be wondered at that our best service is given when we are most receptive to His wisdom. We deliver His word most faithfully when we are so pure and naked in intent that we colour His truth with as little of our own emotional accretions and prejudices as possible.

Yet, as we have already seen, the Spirit of God does not merely use the counsellor as a mouth-piece. On the contrary, the counsellor's life and witness are part of the spirit of counsel. In all spiritual transactions the human role is as important as that of God. He initiates the work, but it is our privilege and responsibility to execute it:

> Unless the Lord build the house,
>   its builders will have toiled in vain.
> Unless the Lord keeps watch over a city,
>   in vain the watchman stands on guard.
> In vain you rise up early and go late to rest,
>   toiling for the bread you eat;
> he supplies the need of those he loves.
>
> (Ps. 127:1-2)

If we are to play our part in the world's work, and especially in its deliverance from the law of decay to the glory of transfiguration, we must be constantly open to the inspiration of the Holy Spirit who speaks not on His own authority, but tells us only what He hears (John 16:13). The message is from the Father, from Whom He proceeds and from the Son to whose glory He is the agent as well as the witness. 'He will glorify me, for everything that he makes known to you he will draw from what is mine. All that the Father has is mine, and that is why I said, "Everything that he makes known to you he will draw from what is mine".' (John 16:14-15).

The work of discernment has two faces; the ability to establish the source and authority of one's own inner guidance and counsel, and the power to assess and direct the guidance that emanates through the lives of other people. For if the guidance is aberrant, the lives of those who rely on its directing power will founder on the rocks of illusion and mischievous misdirection. If the guidance is, on the other hand, of noble quality and strict logic, it will bring all those with whom the person communicates into creative psychic fellowship with him and indeed with all life.

In our unenlightened state we believe that our mind is the source and foundation of all knowledge that issues from us and is translated into words of wisdom. This human wisdom is, in fact, an amalgam of tradition handed on to us and the prejudice that rises up from our own unconscious mind. It speaks to the condition of those who share our unenlightenment and are full of unquestioned assurance, and it serves merely to confirm past attitudes and established ways of thinking. Furthermore, apparently autonomous, or self-governing, sources of information and direction may impinge themselves on the conscious mind, so that the person is led in a new way, sometimes with dictatorial force. These autonomous sources of direction that appear to take over the personality may claim a god-like authority, and threaten the person – and those whom he may be impelled to instruct according to the message he has received – with dire consequences if the word is not obeyed. In this way the individual becomes increasingly dominated by the source of information that wells up within him and at the same time overwhelms him from beyond himself, so that his life is spent largely in appeasing a menacing, nameless power that assumes a divine role. This power takes its origin from a split-off part of the personality, or perhaps several such split-off parts, that have never been effectively acknowledged either by the person's family when he was still a child or by himself when he reached adulthood. That which remains unacknowledged, whether it resides in the individual psyche or is a shattered, divided member of the society in which it lives, will wreak its havoc on the body of which it is a rejected member, as it appropriates its measure of life that is given by the Holy Spirit. Nothing can ever be rejected, nor can anything be finally destroyed, however evil we may judge it to be. Everything in existence owes its being to the Creator of all things, Whose nature is love and Whose purpose is redemption and sanctification. Therefore nothing in creation is so small that it can be ignored or too insignificant to be acknowledged. This is the supreme law of relationships, that all things have their place in the one body. And if their place is badly tended and abhorrent to behold, it must be swept up, cleaned and made a haven of welcome by the remainder of the body of God.

Until this is achieved, the aberrant member will assert a private directive force and wreak havoc among the remainder of his brethren. The person who is the victim of this idiosyncratic source of misinformation will be driven to superstitious rituals in order to placate it. Superstition is an irrational regard for a power or force that appears to transcend the natural order and is of a potentially menacing quality. That there are such powers which are outside the natural law depends on our grasp of that law; I believe that if the human were more spiritually based he could aspire to an understanding of the psychic realm that is at present denied him. As we have already seen, the gifts of the Holy Spirit are mediated psychically, and some of them, notably those of healing and manifesting miraculous powers, far exceed anything that can be explained in terms of contemporary science. It would seem that the barriers of time and space which limit our rational view of the world can be penetrated during moments of illumination, when reality is known as the unity of all things in God. But the power of the Holy Spirit is beneficent, inspiring and of great love. Like the father having compassion on his children, so has the Lord compassion on all who fear Him, for He knows how we are made, He knows full well that we are dust (Ps. 103:13–14). By comparison, a frankly malicious psychic source that assumes power over a person's life – whether that source has its origin from within his own psyche, which is the usual condition, or whether it invades his psyche from the vast psychic realm that both transcends and embraces all individual consciousness, in this respect being akin to the collective unconscious described by Carl Jung – is dictatorial, cruel and without compassion on the one it dominates. Alternatively, it may exalt him for a time so as to delude him into thinking he is very important and his message is vital for the future of mankind. As a consequence he feels superior to other people and pities their ignorance and unadvanced state of consciousness. This alternating swing between exaltation and euphoria on the one hand and tyrannical coercion leading to insecurity and naked terror on the other is the way in which a person possessed by an alien psychic entity has his power of private judgment gradually sapped and annulled. The end is enslavement to irrational forces that demolish his power of judgment and his place in society as a responsible, caring member. He becomes increasingly isolated from the fellowship of his peers and the inspiration of the Holy Spirit. He slowly descends into hell, which is most convincingly visualised as an atmosphere of total separation from all sources of relationship, while his awareness of his own dereliction remains until it assumes a terrifying intensity.

There are, however, all grades of sources acting apparently from within the personal psyche that offer inner guidance. The most perfect of these powers is the divine spark; this is the Word of God that is also the light of men (John 1:4). It is the power of Christ in each of us that illuminates the human spirit and is the hope of a glory to come (Col. 1:27). The most terrifying are the aberrant, demonic powers, which we have already considered, that lead, if unchecked, to a total disintegration of the personality. In between these two extremes of sanctity and horror there are psychic entities of an indeterminate nature that are regularly tapped during spiritualistic seances and may occasionally impinge themselves on the psyche of naturally sensitive people even if they have not meddled in occult matters. These are somewhat more difficult to assess, but in the main their spiritually indifferent nature becomes increasingly clear to the disinterested observer as their works show themselves in the lives of those who follow their direction.

It is not unusual in the experience of a spiritual counsellor to encounter a person who is suddenly impelled to take down in writing messages that purport to derive from an impressive personage now inhabiting the world of the life beyond death. These messages may give details about this future existence that we all no doubt are destined to experience after our own death. Sometimes they contain precognitive shafts of information that may be confirmed at a later date in the life of the person who is the amanuensis of the source of direction, or else in the life of one of his (or, more likely, her) associates. The moral and spiritual content of these messages may be quite unexceptionable, stressing the usual concerns of a virtuous person and extolling the practice of honesty, devotion and loyalty. But they are tediously repetitive and do not in any way inspire the person who is controlled by the source of direction to realise those qualities in his own life. Furthermore, they tend to encroach with increasing intensity on the private life of the person, so that he feels he is bound by a sacred duty to lay himself open to the messages and to be completely obedient to their author. Eventually forecasts of coming events are made that are not substantiated.

It seems probable that, at least on some occasions, the source of this indifferent information is the mind-soul complex of a person who has survived death and is inhabiting an astral realm in a purgatorial state. Such a 'discarnate entity' tends to obsess a sensitive person's mind, and may well reactivate and use split-off portions of that individual's own personality. In the realm of psychical research it is generally agreed that the 'control' operating through the medium and bringing what purport to be messages from deceased friends and relatives is a sub-personality of that medium. It may well be in contact with psychic sources beyond the limitation of the time-space realm in which we live our mortal lives.

Interesting as all this may be on the level of theoretical psychology, as a phenomenon directing the lives of people it is untrustworthy and ultimately deleterious. It consumes an increasing amount of time that could be more usefully spent in service and prayer, and it insidiously saps the will and initiative of the person, who is gradually anchored to the very demanding regime imposed by the entity. The entity is, in all probability, not so much evil as misdirected, and it needs release and redirection. The nearest scriptural parallel to this situation is described in the Acts of the Apostles where St Paul and his entourage were followed by a slave-girl who was possessed by an oracular spirit which was a source of great financial profit to her owners. The spirit shouted through her, 'These men are servants of the Supreme God, and are declaring to you a way of salvation.' The girl did this day after day, until Paul could bear it no longer. Rounding on the spirit, he said, 'I command you in the name of Jesus Christ to come out of her', and it went out there and then (Acts 16:16–18).

The interesting feature of this spirit is that it recognised Christ, inasmuch as it extolled Paul and his friends as servants of God and commended their way as one of salvation. In this respect, we come back again to St John's warning about testing the spirits to see whether they are of God. This spirit might quite possibly have affirmed that Jesus Christ had come in the flesh, but it would not have led anyone who heard its message into the way of Christ. On the contrary, by its repetitive proclamation it would more likely have alienated the casual listener from a serious commitment to the one whom it proclaimed. Jesus himself deprecated 'vain repetitions', or a constant babble of words, when one prays to God (Matt. 6:7). What is required is a needle-sharp attention to the voice of the Holy Spirit within one, and an apposite response in words, either spoken or else mentally articulated, to the message one has received. The voice of the Spirit of God within one, in this respect, is usually a silent recognition and resolve that fills one with renewed awareness and dedication; it is much less often an audible directive which one is to follow. Indeed, audible voices within one have to be tested very rigorously to see whether they are authentically of God or come from some diseased psychological state or aberrant psychic source, such as we have already considered.

A message that is authentically spiritual and directed from the Holy Spirit may also come in words; the great prophetic literature of the Old Testament is an immortal record of God's communication with man. The prophetic voice is direct, honest in that it does not flatter the listener or seek to ingratiate itself with him, succinct and morally enlightening. It comes, like the Spirit, blowing where it wills, so that no one can predict its course, let alone control it (John 3:8). The voice comes only when it is necessary for it to be heard, and it leaves the person whose burden and privilege it is to transmit it free at other times. But that person has to devote himself to prayer and following the requirements of the spiritual life. These include honesty in material matters, integrity in personal relationships, and loyalty and renunciation in the service of mankind as a whole. The key word is chastity, a willed continence and a purity and simplicity of taste in all actions, words and thoughts.

When one is the dedicated servant of the Lord, one's life is given over more fully to His service, until the life one lives is no longer one's own life but the life that Christ lives in one, to quote St Paul (Gal. 2:19) for a third time. This means that the superficial, ego-centred life of mortal man, which we all live in our unenlightened moments, has to fall away and be replaced by a life of self-denial in service to God and His creatures. But in losing the ego-directed life we come to a knowledge of the self within that partakes of eternity, since its span is not limited by the time-space world of rational consciousness. No prophet of Israel demonstrates this truth more convincingly than Jeremiah, whose private relationship with the God he served so selflessly was often one of searing complaint and rebellion. 'Lord, I will dispute with thee, for thou art just; yes, I will plead my case before thee. Why do the wicked prosper and traitors live at ease?' (Jeremiah 12:1), and again, 'Alas, alas, my mother, that you ever gave me birth! A man doomed to strife, with the whole world against me. I have borrowed from no one, I have lent to no one, yet all men abuse me' (Jeremiah 15:10). To which God replies: 'If you will then turn back to me, I will take you back and you shall stand before me. If you choose noble utterance and reject the base, you shall be my spokesman' (verse 19). Jeremiah's prophetic work estranges him from nearly all his friends, the scribe Baruch being a notable exception, and God tells Jeremiah that all he can look forward to is service with the Most High. There are no worldly benefits in store for him, as his tragic life story unfolds up to his disappearance with the rebels into Egypt, where he was carried away by them after the fall of Jerusalem, and where presumably he died.

If one is a servant of God one grows in spiritual grace; the message ennobles the prophet and those who have the courtesy and wisdom to heed it. The message from the Holy Spirit sums up the moral climate of the age, at least in the society to which the prophet addresses himself, and it denounces hypocrisy and aberrations fearlessly and categorically. But it also shows the way towards regeneration and healing. It is seldom directed to a single person only – unless that person is a representative of the society in which the prophet works – but it speaks to the condition of all who are addressed. Furthermore, its dire predictions will be fulfilled unless the message is taken to heart and a new direction forged by the chastened wills of those who have heard. The fear of the Lord is the beginning of wisdom, but this fear is one of awe, reverence and burning regard that is more akin to dedication and love than to terror and dismay. This terror, based on the fear of annihilation if the voice is not obeyed, is much more typical of the malicious or morally indifferent psychic entity that possesses the sensitive person and perverts his whole life towards servile compliance and superstitious ritual. The prophet grows into the stature of a full person seen most perfectly in Jesus Himself and foreshadowed by Jeremiah. The transmitter of false prophecy emanating from a psychic source becomes distressingly ego-centred, and his personality becomes coarse and clamant, as is apparent to any disinterested observer. Unfortunately the group of disciples that trail after him remain blind to this moral and spiritual decline, while they become increasingly seduced by vain promises and heretical teachings.

The history of the various cults that are based on idiosyncratic teachings transmitted by a self-appointed leader and the occult groups that hang on the utterances of entranced mediums emphasises the vast difference of their end-product when it is compared with that of the heights reached by the authentic spiritual traditions of the world, enshrined in the great religious faiths. Mysticism and prophecy are the two authentic products of human communion with God. Mystical experience brings the individual who has known as much of the reality of God's unifying presence as it is in the human capacity to bear, into a state of Christ-like renunciation and service for his future work. Prophecy brings the divine message down to the world where it may reconcile fathers to sons and sons to fathers like Elijah, who has always to come before the Lord reveals Himself to subsequent generations lest there is a terrible cosmic destruction (Mal. 4:6).

To bring these thoughts down to the counselling situation, the spirit of discernment works best when we are silent, still and alert. The cloud of unknowing occludes all worldly wisdom, so that we may be enveloped in the divine presence that lies both within us and yet transcends all mortal concepts, while the cloud of forgetting separates us from the emotional anguish and the corruption of thought that find their origin in past prejudice. In this state of complete dedication to the Most High we can listen effectively through the spirit of discernment to what is said, while at the same time sensing the psychic emanations that issue from the person who speaks. These, even more than the rational content of his words, afford a deep measure of the person's integrity and reliability.

Spiritual discernment, though never denying the reason, moves beyond its inevitable limitations. In fact, if our rational faculty is to grow into maturity, it has to learn sufficient humility to be able to renounce its secure seat of dogmatic authority and be open to new insights. These come to us psychically from our communication with other living sources through the power of the Holy Spirit. The spirit of discernment will recognise and analyse the various 'spirits' obsessing the mind of the disturbed patient or the self-styled prophet, as the case may be. It is in this way that the intuition is developed; this is the faculty of rapid, concise and accurate assessment of a situation without prior knowledge of the pertinent facts from which a rational deduction could have been made. The succinct assessment is succeeded by positive action to heal or to remove foreign interference, as the circumstances may indicate.

The possibility of psychic invasion by foreign, hostile powers or entities was taken for granted in the time of Jesus, and is also accepted by many peoples who are dismissed out of hand by the sophisticated world as primitive, even uncivilised. On the whole, this suspicious attitude towards the possibility of invading psychic forces is soundly based, but it is accepted too dogmatically by modern psychological theory and practice. It is certainly much more convenient and plausible to attribute all mental abnormality to a breakdown in the person's own mind, usually as a result of dysfunction of his brain. But, in fact, living systems are more complex than this, and it is the rule that any disease or disturbance of human function is likely to have a number of factors involved in its causation.

One of the primary principles of scientific research is to seek always for the least complicated explanation, in order to keep things as simple as possible. This principle of simplification works by cutting away all unnecessary hypotheses using what is called Occam's razor, William of Occam being the mediaeval scholar who first enunciated the principle. This approach to truth works best in inorganic systems, but progressively less well in the more evolved living species, of which the human is the most complex, at least in our world. Admittedly in any human disease there is presumably a primary or principal cause, but to it there are added in most cases a number of precipitating or contributory factors which may, for instance, be genetic, environmental, psychological, social or psychic. This is simply a tribute to the complex nature of living forms who, far from being isolated units, thrive in close contact with their fellows, alternatively in co-operation and rivalry, in accord and destructive fury.

Those who are psychically sensitive can often detect the presence of foreign forces, or entities, in some localities. These may be, and indeed usually are, memory traces of past events that occurred in those premises; they are comparable in their way to the aroma that may persist in certain places, except that a psychic residue can persist indefinitely unlike a physical marker that wanes rapidly with the passing of time. On other occasions the entities appear to be a part of the personality of someone who once frequented the place in his physical body. Such a personality is described as earth-bound, and needs to be moved on to his further destination which God alone knows. All this is not surprisingly dismissed as superstitious nonsense by those of obtuse sensitivity, who live in an insulated, self-centred edifice but do not effect deep relationships with other people. Perhaps they are the most fortunate, for they at least remain oblivious of and impervious to a great deal of the emotional turmoil and naked evil that interpenetrate the collective psyche of our species! But this insensitivity excludes such people from the heights of many of the most important experiences in life, whether aesthetic, altruistic, heroic or mystical. To know these fully, one has to quit the little citadel of the ego, so safe and reassuring, and enter the boundless tracts of one's own psyche which is in limitless communion with the collective psyche of the human race and no doubt with much more besides this. This is the way of counsel by which the spirit of discernment develops in mastery.

That the psyche of highly sensitive people, especially those who are already psychiatrically ill with a known mental disorder and those who meddle unwisely in psychic matters, may be obsessed or even possessed by discarnate forces is again well recognised by those with special gifts of discernment. These gifted people are, in my experience, rare.

In this treacherous and highly nebulous realm there are obsessional believers in spirit possession just as in the mental sciences generally there are the great majority who dismiss the possibility of possession out of hand, indeed impugning the sanity of anyone who shows any sympathy towards such a belief. The truth lies somewhere between these two extremes, with the bias heavily weighted in favour of the agnostic viewpoint. It is extremely unlikely that a mentally and emotionally healthy person would ever be invaded by an extraneous psychic source. Therefore it can be assumed that the potential victim is already seriously deranged, thereby being rendered all the more vulnerable to psychic assault. Likewise the type of person who is obsessively drawn to private psychic exploration is usually emotionally abnormal – his delight in the occult is a way of relieving his feelings of inferiority in his daily work, so that he can bask in a self-constructed fantasy world of 'gnosis' reserved for initiates into secret mysteries and arcane, man-made societies. That such secret orders may possess some psychic knowledge is conceivable, but it is seldom deep and nearly always deleterious to those in contact with it. This is because it is used selfishly for personal ends even if service to others is proclaimed. Like attracts like in the world of relationships, and the entities attracted to this debased type of usage are on the dark, sinister verge. We have already considered how such an obsessed person gradually surrenders his integrity, becoming enslaved to destructive forces, and ending up in a hell-like state of isolation.

In dealing with this situation, the person who may be psychically invaded must be investigated initially by the established psychiatric and psychotherapeutic agencies. As we have noted, such people are already mentally abnormal, and even if an infesting psychic power is involved, they still need specialised psychiatric care. The entity will not be displaced so long as the victim clings on to it. Only when he seeks help and is prepared to face his past life with its devious problems in an attitude of sober responsibility can an attempt be made to dislodge an invading force. This should be done preferably by a minister of religion using the authority implicit in his ordination, and here there must be both belief in the transcendent power of God and the authenticity of the orders under which the minister functions. Such an entity has to be commanded to quit its present unsatisfactory abode in the name of God, and directed to seek God's forgiving help so as to come to its rightful place in the life beyond death. Minor degrees of obsession can be dealt with by a psychically sensitive lay person, but it is certain that the authority of an ordained minister is essential for more dangerous work. He should, in any case, be protected by the prayers of many concerned people; religious communities can play an especially valuable part in this work of protective prayer. The same basic approach is appropriate for haunted premises. The use of consecrated water is recommended as is also the Eucharist if the circumstances are appropriate. The minister of deliverance, a more fortunate title than exorcist because it is less negative in approach to the discarnate entity, learns the way through his own experience and the guidance of the Holy Spirit.

It should always be stressed that the possibility of psychic invasion does not deny the reality of personal responsibility. The invasion would not have occurred had the person not been open to it. It is for this reason that our way of life and the control we have over our thoughts and actions are most important. Promiscuity in relationships, notably sexual ones, lays the person especially open to psychic invasion; this applies also to drug abuse and alcoholic excess. People who live their lives in chastity and order are not liable to infestation by dark forces. The Holy Spirit is a spirit of order and discipline. He produces remarkable phenomena, but these serve to inspire us to a higher calling and a more selfless love of others. St Paul reminds us that the fruits of the Holy Spirit are love, joy, peace, patience, kindness, goodness, fidelity, gentleness and self-control (Gal. 5:22). He may be a hard taskmaster, but the Holy Spirit always leads us into the full exercise of our humanity, a humanity to be measured by nothing less than the humanity of God the Son. The fruits of invading forces potentiate the natural corruptibility of our unredeemed lower nature – they do not so much add new perversions as unmask and emphasise the weaknesses already present. St Paul's list again cannot be improved: fornication, impurity, indecency, idolatry, sorcery, quarrels, a contentious temper, envy, fits of rage, selfish ambitions, dissensions, party intrigues, jealousies, drinking bouts and the like (Gal. 5:20). People who live squalid lives deny the high calling of a human being, and are open to the dark elemental forces of the collective unconscious that seek to bring all creation back to the primal chaos from which it was fashioned by God's great creative act.

There can be little doubt that the spirit of discernment is a high attribute of God's spirit of counsel set upon us as a mark of distinction. To bear it the life of the counsellor must be one of self-giving discipline to the Most High.

9.

Counselling towards Liberation

'Man is born free but is everywhere in chains' was an assessment of the human condition made some two hundred years ago by Jean-Jacques Rousseau. He was the chief protagonist of the 'back to nature' movement that had such a profound social and political effect in the late eighteenth century and which played an important part in precipitating the French Revolution. The chains that anchor the spirit of man in incarceration are, in the first analysis, external, environmental ones. Our social and educational conditioning determines in no small measure how we shall respond to life's call, whether we shall affirm our identity and move courageously into the dark future or whether we shall deny life's challenge and retire defeated before we start the race into some obscure backwater where we can hide ourselves. Here we may either live parasitically on others or else simply rail against the unfairness of our lot and vent jealous hatred on all those who seem to attain success in life.

But the root of our enslavement and imprisonment is much deeper than this. It is related to the divided consciousness that we carry along with us. We bear the seeds of failure and disappointment with us from an early age, due in good measure to the inadequate love and acknowledgment we received when we were very young. This topic we have already considered earlier in connection with the building up of a significant ego-consciousness. Many people who come for help and counsel bear the incubus of failure decisively upon their psyche; even before they make an application for some employment they know they will be rejected because the pattern of failure and rejection is part of their life history and is ingrained on them heavily and inexorably. In due course, this negative psychological approach is made manifest in emotional disturbance and bodily dysfunction. 'Where there is no vision, the people perish' (Prov. 29:18); this famous aphorism is appropriate to the individual in his response to life no less than to the group and nation. An intolerable incubus of negative feelings weighs down the psyche and prevents the leaping forward of the spirit within the soul. It is thus that the healthy human being responds to the call of the Holy Spirit and dares to obey the summons it issues to live creatively and joyously. Anyone involved in the work of counselling will come across this negative type of client with depressing frequency. In the end it is the faith of the counsellor that will ignite the damp wick of the client's lamp, so that a conflagration may eventually issue forth from his soul.

In coming to terms with negative feelings that thwart our life and place a dampening heaviness on all new associations that might otherwise open up fresh vistas of hope in the darkened mind, we have first to review our own past. The psychoanalytic process may often be of considerable value in leading all concerned to the origin of the trouble, which usually, at least in my experience, stems from some dramatic termination of a vital relationship very early in a child's life. One who acknowledged the worth and uniqueness of the small child had been taken away abruptly, and without explanation or compassion, and something of comparable strength and durability had not been substituted. The little one finds he lacks a secure base, and is therefore liable to be blown in all directions by powerful forces that play around him and over which he has no control. He does not act consecutively under the challenge of these psychic surges, but is sucked in passively, so that his freedom is brutally disregarded and destroyed, and the power of his will vitiated.

In fact, when we consider the vast indifferent forces that play around us in the brief life we spend in this world, it is remarkable that so many of us survive, let alone flourish, as indeed we do. Even in privileged Western societies the pressure against the individual actualising his own true identity, so that he may become a person in his own right, is very considerable. It has been said with cynical realism that if one wants to prosper in this strange life one should start by choosing the right parents. This applies not only to their genetic endowment but also to the position they hold in the world and the impetus their wealth and prestige can give in launching their offspring on to a favourable start in life's race. But even this apparent truism is not entirely correct: highly successful parents can cramp the style of their offspring, making their achievements appear bare and negligible in comparison with their own. Indeed, famous men seldom have successful, fulfilled children. Not only is it hard for the candle to shine in the presence of a blazing orb, but the celebrity also tends to steal the limelight to the diminishment of those compelled to live in his proximity. The concern a more ordinary type of parent might bestow on his children is dissipated prodigally in the attention given to the admirers and sycophants that block the path of the famous one. Indeed, the person who is to make a real name for himself, a name of the measure of the One Whose name is above every name, to Whom every knee shall bow, has to establish his own identity as soon as possible and to forge a path independently of the vogues and fashions of the world around him. This is what liberation is about, the freedom of the individual to become a person.

In the process, there has to be an increasing insight into the depths of one's own previous bondage, and this, as we have already stated, requires some analytic discipline. The first analyst is the Holy Spirit, and if one is mentally and emotionally stable one can bear His insistent thrust towards the confrontation of the truth about oneself without the assistance of a human counterpart. That one's unconscious may be made fully conscious is the implicit prayer of a person passionately dedicated to the spiritual path. It is perhaps the most terrible of prayers, because what may be revealed is at times scarcely bearable; here the support of a therapist-counsellor can indeed be invaluable. But such a counsellor has to know the contours of the inner life very well if his presence is not to be an incubus rather than a support. Only one who has borne the wounds of suffering and has emerged battered but regenerated can offer much practical help to the person seeking liberation.

This liberation leads to the abandonment of old ways of thought and long-established attitudes that cripple one as one approaches a new situation even before one's steps are finally laid. This release from the bondage of the past depends on faith which is confirmed in action and fertilised with courage. One popular method of attaining, or at least attempting to attain, a reversal of past negative attitudes is the practice of positive thinking. St Paul says, 'All that is true, all that is noble, all that is just and pure, all that is lovable and gracious, whatever is excellent and admirable – fill your thoughts with those things' (Phil. 4:8). An even more basic way of reversing a tendency towards personal subversion and demoralisation is by visualising oneself in a role of success and happiness. What is placed assiduously in the imagination eventually influences the will, and finally the longed-for action may become a reality. Likewise, if one affirms a statement often enough, one comes to believe it and then to act upon it. The sinister aspect of this psychological truth is much used by propagandists of totalitarian regimes among the broad population to inculcate hatred against minority groups whom it is intended to destroy. If an untruth is circulated against a particular ethnic or social group, it will come to be believed by sheer repetition, and soon those who are the victims of hatred will be attacked and destroyed by the ignorant indoctrinated population.

In fact, however, a person with a negative view of himself of such a magnitude that he expects failure as the only certainty in his life, is unlikely to be converted to a more positive attitude towards the future by simply being told that he is really an excellent person with great potentialities. This is the rule even if the assessment is factually correct and not merely an exercise of kindly, but blurred, compassion. Self-denigration, with its terrible corollary of a wish for death and destruction is too deep-seated to be expunged merely by facile, though sincere, words. What is needed is a much deeper concern that issues forth in love. Great love alone can effect a lasting change in a person's image of himself, whereas flowery language repels by its apparent superficiality. This love cannot simply be contrived; if it were, its shallowness would soon become so apparent that the one in need would flinch from it. The love comes from God, Who changes all things and makes them new. It is thus that we enter into a fresh regard for ourselves and experience the balm of freedom.

It follows that the way of liberation from crippling fear, self-denigration and hopelessness is once again that of silent communion. It is in the stillness of self-giving that the essential psychic commitment is established between the counsellor and the client. What is achieved in this creative silence is an atmosphere of trust, so that eventually the barriers that separate the soul of the one in need may be lowered sufficiently for him to communicate effectively with the counsellor, and as time goes by with an increasing range of his fellows also. As the shuttered soul is opened to the light of God's love, so the analytic prowess of the Holy Spirit can bring the receptive, now encouraged, mind of the client into clearer perception. This renewed mind can focus on the past with less emotional pain, and begin to come to terms with itself and its unconscious elements more decisively.

What caused the self-destructive attitude to life with its attendant depression and impotence is, on the level of theory, of great interest. Some therapists blame early childhood experiences, others events that were registered by the foetus while in its mother's womb, so that the maternal disposition was relayed to the embryo even immediately after its conception, while the most extreme attribute many present problems to events that occurred in a past life. Suffice to say that, while these last two theories are of compelling interest, they as yet lack that scientific substance which alone would convince the more agnostic among us. But in the end, even if the cause of the malign attitude to life which clouds any enjoyment and darkens all pleasant anticipation with gloom and foreboding is elucidated with certainty, this understanding in itself is unlikely to effect a dramatic change in the client's attitude. The negative response to any new trail or endeavour has become so ingrained that all new ventures and opportunities will continue to be subverted by the divided mind.

One way of altering this pre-ordained negativity is the use of the power of suggestion, including the repetition of positive thoughts, as we have already noted. But until there is a radical change in the deeper, inner consciousness of the person, these thoughts will not penetrate the heart, and will continue to have a negligible effect on his life style and relationships with other people. It is the faith transmitted psychically, and later on intellectually also, that begins to change the previously immutable face of the soul. From its surface the rays that emerge from the spirit within it may shine forth and begin to integrate the entire personality around that central focus within. This is the individual spirit, which in turn is energised and directed by the Holy Spirit.

Faith is, in essence, an openness to the creative potentiality of life and does not require a detailed credal affirmation. In terms of the Christian revelation, that creative potentiality was made manifest in the Incarnation of the Word of God, Who brings healing and sanctification to all who are willing to receive Him. This He does by the power of the Creator Spirit who is eternally making all things new (Rev. 21:5). The faith that gives meaning to the endeavours, indeed the life, of the counsellor, is that there is a positive value in living, that all things have in them the capacity to bring good in the lives of those to whom they show themselves, even if their first appearance is forbidding, unpleasant and even disastrous. The statement of hope in Romans 8:18, that the sufferings we now endure bear no comparison with the splendour, as yet unrevealed, which is in store for us, is the watchword of the faith of all spiritual counselling. It is based neither on scriptural fundamentalism nor on wishful thinking that subtly evades the dark, menacing issues of life. It is related to the sense of quickening in the soul that responds in eager expectation to the challenge of life as a new thing is revealed, as the gestation of God's providence is brought to the light of day in a fresh creation, soft and beautiful, invigorating and restoring. This faith that affirms that all things work together for good for those who love God (Rom. 8:28) is the essence of the psychic thrust that heals. It is the spearhead that drives the power of the Holy Spirit deep into the shivering, clammy flesh and cowering mind of the afflicted one and illumines his whole personality with God's uncreated light. From this stems the healing power of the Holy Spirit, and a fresh glimpse of reality then informs the previously diffident, hopeless individual, who can at last respond positively with a strengthened, vigorous will.

The counsellor shows this faith not so much in speech as in wordless communion. What one is as a person flows out from one psychically so that even a child or a mentally defective person can appreciate the solicitude and authority that informs the work of the devoted minister of healing. When a relationship of trust has been established, only then can one offer the person one's support and affirm its constancy. At this stage the psychological techniques associated with positive thinking can be used. The main work is to arouse the client's interest, so that the black, dank apathy disappears and is replaced by a lively commitment in the new work that eventually blossoms into willing service. One has to forget oneself if one's work is to be of the greatest value and also if one is to be accepted unconditionally by other people. This is a very practical application of Jesus' dictum, 'The man who loves himself is lost, but he who hates himself in this world will be kept for eternal life. If anyone serves me, he must follow me; where I am my servant will be. Whoever serves me will be honoured by my Father' (John 12:25-6).

The self that is loved by the superficial man is the ego-nature suitably adorned by the finery of wealth, worldly success and the esteem of others. Only when that superficial self is left behind can the Spirit within, that of Christ Who is our hope of a glory to come, be encountered, and the person move from the limitations of this world that ends in death and enters into a present knowledge of eternity. In this knowledge he forgets his ego and its demands; instead he serves God to the exclusion of all else. In God's service alone is the perfect freedom to be oneself, since He knows us as we are, and does not need to be impressed by our cleansed image. We remember, of course, that Jesus, like all spiritual teachers expounding the way of life, speaks in vigorous hyperbole. The denunciation of self-love and the commendation of self-hatred is an emphasis on the radical nature of one's submission to God's service – which is always extended to the service of one's fellow men. When I cease to think about myself but can accept myself for what I am, and get about God's work, I know of that positive approach to life that alone tells of immediate and everlasting freedom. This indeed is the end of liberation: to be oneself and do the work which has been apportioned to one each moment of life.

In fact, the power of positive thinking is ultimately limiting to the full development of the person. When I am at a low ebb, then assuredly some small success or minor recognition can renew my self-esteem by investing it with a reasoned confidence. But when I am truly in harmony with life and in rhythm with the flow of the cosmos, the necessity for success and recognition fades into the background of my considerations. What matters is the work at hand, the privilege I have of doing it, and its end-product in terms of service to my fellow men. To be able to esteem oneself as a person in one's own right is the beginning of a valid independent existence; to forget oneself completely in the glorious flow of creative activity that pervades the universe is the end of total living.

This is, as we noted previously, the progress from the development of a fully substantiated ego to the establishment of the deep centre in which the spiritual self is known. The creative activity of the universe is the outer thrust of the Holy Spirit, and as one participates in it with selfless abandon, so one knows the spiritual self, the soul within, and its vibrant exultation is a part of the triumphant joy of eternal life. The counsellor who knows this joy in himself will transmit it psychically to those whom he serves. It must be added, as a sober fact of life, that our world is hardly one of joy and exultation on a day-by-day rational basis; the tragedies inevitable to living, stemming both from existence itself and from man's terrible cruelty and aggressiveness, would seem to make spontaneous paeans of praise somewhat insensitive if not simplistic. But the soul knows that in the depths of life there is an eternal spark of God's presence, and this will prevail, indeed triumph, long after the outer façade of destructive fury has spent itself and become dissipated into the mists of insubstantiality. This is a living faith that renews and regenerates all whom it touches.

This faith is of a very different order from the unconscious – and not infrequently crudely conscious – manipulation that may proceed from a particularly enthusiastic counsellor. This enthusiasm is based on the certainty that what he believes and expounds is the whole truth, and that healing depends on his client accepting this approach without reservations or criticism. We all tend to become manipulative when we are sure we know the answers and have the key to the mystery of healing. This dogmatic certainty can even be transmitted psychically to the client, who then conjures up dreams and memories that seem to confirm a specious hypothesis that masquerades as absolute truth. Many such hypotheses, such as the importance of the trauma of past lives (with a reincarnational bias) or of the earliest period of intra-uterine development of the embryo with the uncovering of suggestive memories, may indeed have a substance of truth behind them. But the memories evoked by techniques of regression may simply represent the uncovering of conversations heard and stories read to one at a very early period of one's life.

The psyche dramatises its contents, especially that which was once repressed and is now uncovered. Our dream life is the most eloquent example of this dramatisation of our interior world of ideas, drives and emotions. Their elucidation can be helped by the established canons of interpretation developed by the classical schools of dynamic psychology, especially the Freudian and the Jungian, but in the end the dreamer and the thinker has to come to his own conclusions. Our inner lives are all unique, though in many respects they share common factors of detail and symbolism. A manipulative therapist can easily impose his will and interpretation on to his patient who then follows uncritically in the way shown by the dominating guide. If we are humble, silent and open, we can get ourselves out of the way and let the Holy Spirit show the client what the truth of the matter is that shows itself to him in thoughts, piercing emotional thrusts and evocative dreams.

Dreams function on a number of levels. Most are essentially psychological mechanisms of inner release and instruction. Apart from the surface dreams that are an obvious reaction to an immediate life situation, there are more profound dreams that indicate some unresolved tension in one's inner life or act as a corrective against a conscious over-reaction to some pressing situation or circumstance. There are also much deeper dreams that have a cosmic, mystical significance as well as those that remind us that we do not live alone in a private world but are in psychic communion with all souls, the deceased no less than those still in the flesh with us. Such psychically enlightening dreams may have a strongly precognitive aspect that is suddenly brought to mind later on when it is confirmed by an apparently trivial event in one's life or a more compelling tragedy or triumph that shatters one in its intensity. I personally believe that we can understand aspects of the after-life through instruction that is given by the Communion of Saints by means of deep dreams and that our loved ones on the other side of life can communicate with us on this level. The information that at times can be given seems to me to be far too complex to be a mere projection of one's own inner thoughts. And the emotional release afforded by these glimpses has a sanely liberating effect on one's future life. At any rate they deserve careful consideration and a deep reverence, since they reveal the heart in all its complexities.

It should also be noted that faith and doubt are obverse sides of the same coin. Faith without doubt leads to credulity and irrationality that find their end in crass superstition and the persecution of those who do not share that faith. On the other hand, obsessive doubts paralyse one's initiative and lead one to imprisonment in the status quo which is identified with unalterable reality. If faith is the yearning of the soul for its release from the bondage of materialism to the freedom of full participation in eternal life, then doubt is the mumbled warning of the rational mind that the release yearned for may be the precipice that leads to total destruction. And this is the perpetual conflict lying at the heart of man's aspirations; a knife edge separates annihilation from fulfilment, total obliteration of the personality from a full participation of the person in the divine nature so that he may come to share in the very being of God (2 Peter 1:4).

The spirit of discernment acts primarily through the rational mind, which is especially powerful in the male. But that spirit also acts psychically through the intuition, which is especially strong in the female. While faith leads us on, doubt draws us back from ultimate commitment. The final decision is a resolution of these two attitudes; it is a reconciliation of the two opposing tendencies.

Only when faith and doubt are both given their due regard, and the messages of each are received attentively and with reverence, can the will function in clear awareness and the soul move towards its true destination, which is God. Our faith can be real only when it is viewed before a severe background of doubt. The proof of one's faith is the way one directs one's life in accordance with its precepts. In other words, faith is made real by action. It gives substance to our hopes, and makes us certain of realities we do not see (Heb. 11:1). In fact these realities are already seen by the soul's eye, which is the spirit within us. But what is known to be true by the deepest intuition has to be brought into outer reality in the action of our lives, so that it may transform both our own personalities and the world in which we live. Faith, if it does not lead to action, is in itself a lifeless thing (Js. 2:17). But the action must always first be scrutinised and censored by the mind, which is the advocate of doubt. When enthusiasm has been tempered by doubt, judgment and a considered, well-conceived action will be the result. This will lead us on to the path of life both in eager expectation and in fear and trembling, so that we are ever open to the responses of other people and the directives that arise from new circumstances. These come about in our progress towards full humanity, towards the actualisation of the self into something of the nature of Christ.

Therefore doubt, though stressing the dark, forbidding side of existence, is as much part of the divine providence as is faith. It tempers exuberant recklessness with the stern facts of life, it brings idealism down to earth, making it practical. But in the end, if it is allowed always to have the last word, it truncates the full development of the person, who remains merely an intelligent puppet, and is not allowed to attain his destiny which is to be a spiritual being, one who can know God, obey His high calling and enter into the divine stature of Christ. In doing so he also becomes fully human, in the footsteps of Jesus in His mighty incarnation.

10.

Discipline in the Service of Freedom

Liberation is a steady, slow growth of the person towards the full actualisation of his identity. This identity is separate from the milieu in which he was conceived, born and educated and also from the environment in which he pursues his livelihood in co-operation and conflict with the milling throng around him. As he grows to full spiritual maturity, so he transcends the restraints and limitations of his background and the society in which he lives, and starts to forge his own path away from the monotonous tumult of the crowds who tend to move in restricted circles of vanity. Their vision is usually limited to immediate gratification of the senses; his, on the other hand, extends to include the whole cosmos in its regard. All this, if unqualified, would seem to imply that the actualised person dispenses with all human ties and communal solidarity and moves into a rarefied domain of individualistic spiritual exploration. In fact, it is only when one is liberated from the thralldom of personal attachment, and gives oneself unconditionally to God, that one can begin to relate constructively to the people around one and the society one has been called on to serve.

Jesus had no doubt where the fulfilled person's priority lay: it lay with God, so that it might aid in the resurrection of the world. Our progressive movement into freedom starts with our emancipation from inner fears and negative attitudes to life, a liberation effected by the spirit of love and faith given to us by God, often through the agency of a spiritually aware friend or counsellor. The next part of personal freedom involves a loosening of obsessive ties with other people, whose favourable opinion of one is essential for one's own self-esteem. Indeed, we cannot know real freedom until we have parted with our reputation in the service of truth. It is more liberating for me to appear a complete failure in the eyes of my colleagues by being true to my own insights than to glow in the esteem of others while denying my own identity, known in terms of the soul's response to moral values. 'What does a man gain by winning the whole world at the cost of his true self?' (Mark 8:36). The time spent in the wilderness is a crucially formative period in the lives of many great creative artists. It is even more significant in the growth into authenticity that punctuates spiritual mastery. It is in this spirit that Jesus' radical criticism of wealth finds its most important application: a person can no more enter the kingdom of heaven while encumbered with the adornments of money, power or intellectual prowess than can a camel pass through a needle's eye (Mark 10:25). To be liberated from the need for this world's riches is to move from an uncertain identity that depends on our outer reputation to an enduring identity that radiates from within us as a seal of our integrity.

We have also to break loose from long-established attitudes of mind and limiting ways of thought. On one occasion Jesus invited someone to follow Him, but the man first wanted to bury his father. Jesus told him to leave the dead to bury their dead, but that he should go and announce the kingdom of God (Luke 9:59–60). On another occasion, the man invited wanted first to bid farewell to his family, to which Jesus replied that no one who sets his hand to the plough and then keeps looking back is fit for the kingdom of God (Luke 9:61–62). Clearly, the disposal of the dead and a proper caring leave-taking, perhaps for good, of those close to one, is mandatory. But first there must be a full commitment to God. If one sets one's mind on God's kingdom and His justice before everything else, the rest will come to one as well (Matt. 6:33). In other words, in the two situations described above, if the would-be disciples had declared their allegiance to Christ first, they would have been able to do the work that filial piety and common duty demanded with the greatest alacrity while serving the Lord. But if the day's work takes precedence over our duty to God, we shall soon become so submerged in worldly care that the light of God will be occluded from our spiritual vision.

The same deficiency results when a person is too busy to find a time for silent communion with God in the practice of contemplation, which is as necessary for the well-being of the inner man as breathing is for the body. Constructive living is largely an exercise in assessing our priorities: only when the spiritual dimension claims our first allegiance can the demands of social, family and personal life be fulfilled and enjoyed. The peace that passes understanding, which is the basis of the faith of the counsellor that all will be well in the end, comes admittedly as a gift from God. But it has also to be cultivated by a disciplined inner life with a controlled outer expression in the various relationships that punctuate our work in the world. To be able to receive requires us first of all to put ourself in a state of stillness and trust. And this discipline of the inner life has to be learnt in slow stages by the client also. On it depends the freedom necessary for a full utilisation of one's gifts and a realisation of one's potential as a human being.

Freedom also involves the body and mind, both so often seduced by physical lust or emotional clinging. The body should be cherished but not indulged, while the mind should be filled with good things but not allowed to enter an undisciplined arena of vain imagining. The act of confession is a most powerful means towards inner healing. That confession may be directly to God in the course of prayer or it may be of the sacramental kind in which a priest pronounces the words of absolution to the shriven penitent, shriven of all his erstwhile conceit and subterfuge by the revealing power of the Holy Spirit who always brings the truth to any situation. A counselling session, and even more so a psychotherapeutic one, is largely concerned with bringing up old attitudes and actions which previously lay dormant in the unconscious, into full remembrance. Here their psychic and emotional charge is experienced to the full, and the impact on the mind may be of overwhelming horror.

St James says, 'The prayer offered in faith will save the sick man, the Lord will raise him from his bed, and the sins he may have committed will be forgiven. Therefore confess your sins to one another, and pray for one another, and then you will be healed' (Js. 5:15–16). The important part of prayer is the faith that accompanies it. As we have already seen, faith is made manifest in action. Once we have been put in right relationship, or justified, with God by faith, that faith will be the basis of the appropriate action. Praying with faith is an offering of the one who prays to make himself a living sacrifice to God's service. Prayer devoid of any commitment to action is a vain thing. God acts primarily through us as human beings in the economy of our world; if we are not prepared to play our part, the divine initiative founders in futility, and nothing is achieved.

In the same way, a confession made without a strong inner commitment that the penitent may change his way of life is essentially futile. It is, in other words, of little use praying for our sins to be forgiven so long as the inner desire to lead a new life and put away old, selfish attitudes of mind is lacking. That desire, if it is real and not merely an exercise of wishful thinking, is consummated in a commitment to serve God and our fellow men. God is served in the practice of prayer, during which we open ourselves in complete, attentive self-dedication to His word, and learn from the depths of our being what He would have us do for our own welfare and that of the world around us. Our fellows are served by an equally intense self-dedication to them and their needs, so that, by the power of God's Spirit, we may learn what they need and then begin to fulfil that requirement, as God shows us.

In all these acts of service, it is the word of God that directs us, and not our own arrogant assurance that we know what is best. This is, in fact, the essence of spiritual counselling compressed into a simple definition: the bringing of God's wisdom down to the hungry populace by the practice of silent attention and selfless devotion. And then an inner healing is effected in which the soul of the client is put into its rightful alignment with God's purpose seen in terms of eternity. This is a very different end from the mere relief of a present indisposition, so that the person may feel better and be more contented and well-disposed to his present situation. While temporary amelioration is in no way to be derided, it is to be seen essentially as psychological first-aid treatment; until the makeshift relief is incorporated into an edifice of deep integrated healing there is the imminent threat of a future breakdown and disintegration of all that was erected so superficially and improvidently. The edifice of deep healing is constructed by the client alone; no one else can do it for him. We have already considered Psalm 127 to the effect that God initiates all human endeavours, but the execution of the work that builds the outer temple of the world is our human responsibility. In fact, the model of the outer temple, where God is worshipped in spirit and truth, is to be found in the light of the spirit within each of us, but what we are shown on the mountain of illumination has to be transposed to the world of material substance. Moses too was told to work to the design which he had been shown on Mount Sinai (Exod. 25:40).

In the work of rebuilding a vibrantly strong personality on the foundation stone that is the spirit within, God is our constant source of inspiration and support. He is aided in the world of spiritual life by the Communion of Saints and the vast Ministry of Angels, of whose existence Elisha was able to enlighten those timid souls who accompanied him in his cleansing mission (2 Kgs. 6:17), and who are with us now also even when our spiritual blindness occludes them from our immediate vision. The counsellor and therapist is a tangible representative of this great concourse of heavenly intelligence, and he can aid mightily in bringing the divine light and wisdom to bear on all immediate human problems. But in the end the client has to commit himself to enter the promised land of freedom and shared responsibility, and this means turning away from the sloth and vicious attitudes of the past and entering by a path of devotion and obedience into a new life. This is to be the forerunner of eternal fellowship with all that exists in God's creative love. The disciplined life that is the only effective way to durable

freedom involves *firstly* the inner way to a knowledge of
God from Whom all freedom comes. Then comes the *second*
part that concerns the individual life of mind and body. All
is consummated in the *third* part which concentrates its
work in relationships with other people. Thus the life of
spiritual discipline consists of contemplation, ascetic living
and purity of relationships. First comes the love of God,
then the loving discipline of oneself, and finally service to
our neighbours, who, as Jesus reminds us in the Parable of
the Good Samaritan, include everyone in immediate
relationship with us.

The greatest act of human discipline is also its most
sublime: a direct confrontation in silence with the hidden
face of God. This is contemplation, which is the zenith of
worship. The basis of worship is giving up everything we
have for the beloved; in essence this means self-renunciation, for each of us is unique in essence and therefore
irreplacable. Our uniqueness is the measure of love that the
Creator has bestowed on us; our self-giving to Him is the
measure of the love received by us from Him which we now
give back, flavoured by our unique presence enhanced by
the spiritual growth which has made that presence a
valuable asset to the world. To contemplate God is to be still
before Him with a clear mind and an attentive will. 'Speak,
Lord; thy servant hears thee' (1 Sam. 3:9–10). In the silence
the Holy Spirit penetrates the psyche, cleansing the rational
faculty and purifying the emotions until the physical body is
itself renewed and healed. Contemplation is both the heart
of prayer and its zenith; it is both the precondition for inner
conversation with God and the end of that conversation.
When we are in one-pointed silent communion with God we
can speak to Him of our sins, our requests, and our concern
for other people. These prayers of confession, petition and
intercession bring our own condition and that of the wider
world into sharp inner focus, and as we pray so we give our
souls and bodies to God as a living sacrifice for the sake of all
the world. We know in that state of self-giving that we are all
parts of the one body, and that as we become filled with
God's Spirit, so we can give that Spirit to all around us,

whether in our daily work or in our silent prayer, which should continue without ceasing if we are living the risen life with Christ. This is indeed the supreme act of spiritual discipline; on it depends not only our effectiveness as counsellors, but also the health and usefulness of our own mind and body.

The life of asceticism is not to be confused with self-torture, when our bodies are mortified for the sake of our souls, allegedly for the good of mankind or our place in the life beyond death. It is, on the contrary, one in which the spirit is alive and vibrant in the personality, so that every disposition of the natural order around us is seen to be invested with new glory and countless possibilities. The ascetic is the spiritual athlete; he trains the body and mind so that they can assist him in his efforts to attain full spiritual mastery. Usually the body is an inert, though voluptuous, incubus to spiritual growth; in this we remember Jesus' words, 'Therefore I bid you put away anxious thoughts about food and drink to keep you alive, and clothes to cover your body. Surely life is more than food, the body more than clothes' (Matt. 6:25). This great counsel of perfect living becomes practical when our minds are lifted up to the hills of aspiration where we may commune with God. In that state of spiritual existence the need for elaborate meals and expensive clothes evaporates. In a barely tangible way the body is filled with something much more essential to its needs even than food. This is the Holy Spirit, and when He is fully with us, our dietary needs are met in that quantity which is best for our health. It is well-known that the affluent tend to eat unwisely and far too much, and that overeating can have very serious effects on the general health, especially of older people, often leading to premature death. When the spirit directs the personality under the guidance of God's Spirit, the body is disciplined in the same way in that the reason is properly focused and the emotions are calmed and channelled into productive avenues of service and understanding.

A trained, disciplined body is a joyous instrument for doing God's work: it witnesses to the vitality of the earth's elements when infused by the Holy Spirit, who gives life and

is its Lord. It is not only our instrument of self-realisation,
but is also a wonderful companion in the day's trials. It
ceases to be the victim of constant or recurrent ill-health
because it is doing its accustomed work smoothly, efficiently
and with an inner awareness of the meaning of its labours.
An unencumbered mind is at the disposal of the person
moment by moment, which can receive, analyse and collate
all information coming to it. It is no longer invaded and
immobilised by extraneous thoughts, but can instead
control all psychic material that enters it from outside.
Under the influence of the spirit the emotions become calm,
tranquil and constructively directed towards the attainment
of what the Holy Spirit reveals. This disciplined calmness
whose end is an attentive listening to the voice within us, so
that we may respond positively and in harmony with the full
flow of the cosmic rhythm around us, is attained only after
much disharmony has been revealed and then released in us.
This indicates the considerable distance that has to be
travelled before the puritan within us (and he is there even in
the hedonist, for we all long for ultimate safety no matter
how much we may spurn it intellectually) matures to the full
stature of the ascetic. The puritan in his full-blooded form
shuns those things that might tempt him away from what he
believes is a course towards God; these diverting agents of
temptation are traditionally classed as the world, the flesh
and the devil. But in the end these apparently subversive
powers are bound to prevail in one form or another. I
personally would go so far as to suggest that it is God's will
that they too should have their hour of triumph, as Satan did
when he reduced Job, that man of blameless and upright life,
to penury and a repulsive skin disease. He who had
previously been a model of affluent piety and holy wisdom
was now less than the dust around him. All that he feared
came upon him (Job 3:25), apparently through meaningless
malice but ultimately for his spiritual emergence into the
realms of transcendent light and eternal love. Had Job,
however, not persevered with the life of holiness before
misfortune struck, it is doubtful whether he would have
passed his great test, for in that test all that was dark in him

was brought to the surface of consciousness as he contended with God in the presence of his three comforters.

Once we have contended with the powers that destroy – and indeed emerged half-dead from the encounter – a new perspective is given us of the life we previously led in blindness and incomprehension. The spirit within us is now known to be the centre of what is real in our lives, and the Spirit of God Who illumines our spirit moves us beyond the slavery of mortal conventions to the freedom of eternal life. The joys of the body, the mind and the emotions are now fully experienced, and that without limit or fear of termination. Now however, the senses no longer yearn for constant stimulation; instead of being slaves to outer sources of diversion and entertainment they assume their rightful place as the instruments by which the world of ultimate reality, eternal nature as some mystics would call it, becomes tangible to us. The gifts of the spirit that God has showered on us, some indeed at the time of our conception, no longer need to be exhibited for our personal glory; instead they assume their rightful place in the scheme of our life by enabling us to play our part in the cosmic flow, whose harmony directs the development of the universe. This harmony is the song of the Holy Spirit as He proceeds unceasingly with His work of renewing the world. To the mystic the song of eternal creation and renewal issues forth as the music of the spheres. One is reminded of God's appearance to Job in that magnificent theophany, when he is asked 'Where were you when I laid the earth's foundations? Who settled its dimensions? Who stretched his measuring-line over it? On what do its supporting pillars rest? Who set its corner-stone in place, when the morning stars sang together and all the sons of God shouted aloud?' (Job 38:4–7). To the contemporary mind, these questions simply reveal the rudimentary state of cosmology of those far-off days. But to the mystic they indicate a grasp of reality that far transcends worldly understanding, for our scientific knowledge is ever-changing, while eternal life proceeds towards the transfiguration of all that is mortal until a new creation emerges, one in which each creature participates consciously in the life of God and of his fellow.

At last we may begin to comprehend the way of discipline that leads to freedom. Early in the spiritual life, the power of decision, of free choice, has to be acknowledged. Here lies our grasp of the will, around which all responsible actions are poised. Once the will is acknowledged as a central focus of the inner life, it has to be trained and strengthened by an assiduous discipline of obedience to the will of God. This obedience consists of the practice of prayer, penance and communal worship. Prayer raises us above our personal concerns to a glimpse of the divine mind, while penance brings us down once more to recollect our selfish attitudes, to remind us how we fail day by day in love to other people. Communal worship may at times be dreary and even unpleasant, but it emphasises in no uncertain way that we too are parts of the one body, which is mankind. When we worship together we give of what we have received in private prayer, and we receive the blessing that comes from the least conspicuous attender, who represents Christ in His humiliation as well as His triumph.

In this way the recalcitrant pleasure-seeking personal will is divested of its selfish preoccupations. It is trained to run the great race of life, and as it proceeds tirelessly in this work, the spirit within is revealed to us. Through that spirit, revealed to us as a centre of peace and light, the Holy Spirit assumes His effortless role of leadership. He moves us to realise our proper humanity which is an image of Jesus' divine humanity. Christ not only releases us from the stultifying domination of our 'lower nature', which is our animal inheritance, but He also leads us to participate fully in the 'higher nature' of God that is a perpetual witness to love and wisdom of a depth far beyond anything this world could grasp. While our lower nature is also a glorious gift, it soon becomes demonic if given precedence so that it is made the measure of a fulfilled person. In fact, our relationship with God is the only true measure of our fulfilment. The lower nature is predatory, striving for its own satisfaction, and heedless of the welfare of other creatures apart from their usefulness to its own ends. The end of this selfish approach to life is death, which is the true wages of sin. But this remorseless process is reversed when the will is awakened and opens itself to God in the abject penitence of prayer. It is then transfigured, and its sights are directed heavenwards. Only then is the lower nature disembarrassed of its lethal dominance, and at once it is also released from the prison of mortality so that it too can glimpse the realm of eternal life that is its inheritance.

The end in store for the flesh is not merely sensual satisfaction, which is inevitably dulled by the inroads of time with its grim harvest of ageing, decay and death. On the contrary, it is the destiny of the ennobled flesh to undergo transfiguration as a prelude to a more widely-embracing resurrection into something of the measure of Jesus' risen body. Resurrection embraces three motions: forgiveness, restoration and exaltation. In this sequence that which was most humiliated is now raised up with Christ beyond death to a knowledge of eternal life. This knowledge is with us even at the present moment when we give ourselves in service to God and our neighbours in self-forgetful devotion. The fruit of the knowledge of eternity is wisdom. If the fear of God is the beginning of wisdom, the end of wisdom is an openness to Him in loving trust. Indeed, the end of the discipline of obedience is this very openness to God's word at all times. From us the word flows out to all those who are available to receive it. Of those people who are receptive to God's wisdom, there is formed the nucleus of a society that can serve humanity in self-giving love and self-transcending wisdom.

The discipline that leads us to freedom is therefore one that reveals the spirit within us. Under the guidance of the Holy Spirit, our own spirit raises up the whole personality from its usual querulous self-assertiveness to a calm self-effacement in service to humanity. It is in this way that we can understand that only in God's service is perfect freedom, because when we are nothing and need to be nothing in terms of the world's esteem, then alone are we truly ourselves as God made us and knows us. Indeed, we are most fully ourselves when we have left our self-regard behind in our service to God, whether in rapt worship or in concern for our fellow creatures in the pursuit of truth, beauty or goodness. This classical platonic triad brings us to the divine footstool in the exercise of the intellectual faculty by which we serve in the world of science, art or philanthropy.

In this spiritual discipline the body learns to limit its demands according to the needs of the whole person rather than to strive for its own satisfaction as an end in itself. It is then the willing servant and not the master of the personality. The mind at the same time acquires the gift of stillness so that it may be attentive to the needs of others and be about its Father's business instead of devising its own schemes and becoming wrapped in its own speculations. The emotions attain a calm compliance instead of issuing a jangled clamour of contrary orders that are to be heeded simultaneously. The end is a truly ascetic life in which the spirit, under the guidance of the Holy Spirit, is unceasingly shepherding the person into a more perfect style of life. In this way we become a vibrant power of renewal for the world about us. We no longer need recognition, but are simply available to assist anyone in need. Constant availability is the fruit of the ascetic life; it means service in joyous abandon without counting the cost. Receiving nothing for oneself – other than the joy of God's eternal presence in one's life – one can give of oneself unstintingly to one's neighbour. The relationship that is articulated in such an encounter is the supreme gift of service freely rendered. In giving, so one receives a blessing from God Himself. The result is that light enters the darkness of the collective human psyche, and resurrection is heralded.

11.

The Counsel of Perfection

At a climactic point in the Sermon on the Mount, Jesus tells His disciples, 'There must be no limit to your goodness, as your heavenly Father's goodness knows no bounds' (Matt. 5:48). He is speaking in the context of love, and His demands are radical: that we should love not only those whom we call our friends, but also those who are evilly disposed towards us, and that we should include them in our prayers. In this respect we remember that God has no favourites, for He loves everything that He has created. Furthermore, love is an absolute quality; it does not have gradations and qualifications, unlike fondness and affection. The measure of love, as we have already seen, is self-renunciation even to death for the sake of the beloved. We see this love in Christ who took the burden of our sin upon Himself, and discharged the odium that He accumulated by death. In that mystery the debt was discharged, and mankind was afforded a new insight into the reality of God as forgiveness replaced guilt and a free pardon was granted to the meanest sinner.

All that was needed was confession – the ability to face the past with dispassionate honesty – and faith to receive the free gift of pardon. The gift comes freely with love – it cannot be earned. But once we have received the gift of love, it will never let us go until all people have been included in its embrace. In this way the faith that saves is proved by the works that heal the world. The proof of love entering our life is that we lose concern for ourself, in its manifest guises of image, reputation, security and rectitude, as we give ourself unstintingly to the one whom we cherish. As I give myself, so I lose myself; as I cease to be the focus of my identity, so the spirit within me shows itself and reveals God's Spirit working within me. Thus Christ lives in me, using my particular qualities and gifts, and I cease to be a separate creature in an impersonal world.

The ultimate freedom is liberation from the demands of the finite personality so that one can participate fully in the life of anyone around one. This is the peak of the counselling process, that one can enter into the personality of anyone who comes for help, and speak to the condition of that person according to the insights given by the Holy Spirit.

Relating to other people is an essential aspect of growing into self-knowledge. One part of understanding ourselves comes with the experience of being alone for some time, when we have to face the usually hidden facets of our character as they come to the surface in the silence. But that understanding is somewhat theoretical until it is practised in the life of the world around us. Self-knowledge is confirmed and substantiated by the responses other people evoke in us, as we in turn bring forth reactions in them. In the exercise of relationships we may experience revulsion and attraction, the one leading us to flee through fear or a sense of deep inferiority, the other drawing us to irrational attachment so that we cannot let the other person free to lead his own life. He becomes an essential part of our sense of identity. But as we progress in life, so we must learn to live in harmony and co-operation with a large number of people, some of whom are closer to us than others. Eventually we have to experience love for at least one person as a presage of the universal love that is to be our final destiny.

The first word in relationships is *respect*, or *courtesy*, for the other person, that he is a being in his own right with his own destiny to fulfil. It is in this frame of mind that we remember Jesus' solemn injunction against judging others, lest we ourselves are judged (Matt. 7:1–2). We have to learn that God's purposes are fulfilled in this world despite outer appearances and even without our approval. The society which is prevalent in many countries at present is permissive almost to the point of carelessness, but one advantage inherent in such a dangerous state of affairs is the freedom for the individual to be himself. What we see we may not like – and *honesty* is the second word in relationships – but we have no right to impress our point of view dogmatically on another person. Jesus reminds us how occluded our own sight is with the beams of self-regard, hypocrisy and a terrible unconcern for others when our own security is under threat. Until these blockages are acknowledged and their removal sought by confession and prayer – for we cannot remove them ourselves by a simple act of will – we are in no position to criticise other people let alone attempt officiously to improve them.

In fact only the practice of non-attached concern can help anyone, and this non-attachment shows itself in leaving the person free to lead his own private life while never ceasing to care for him and be available when he has need of us. In this activity commitment and non-attachment come together. Without non-attachment an attitude of commitment to another person's welfare soon assumes a dictatorial, smothering quality. Non-attachment devoid of commitment on the other hand, soon fades into a clinical detachment in which the person's problems assume a priority over his humanity, so that he is viewed as an interesting case whose progress can teach one much about the natural history of his particular difficulty.

If we encounter each new person with courtesy on the one hand and an honest acceptance of our emotional response to him on the other, we shall begin to form a living relationship with him. The foundation of such a relationship is inner silence so as to listen to what he is saying and sense what lies concealed behind the words. Until we are at peace with ourselves, we cannot be available to receive another person. Listening requires our whole attention, and this cannot be available while we are diverted along some inner track of theorisation, in which we know the answers even before we have heard the problem. Nor can we be available to another person while we are inwardly irritated or fearful, confused or resentful. The result of listening with our undivided attention is the registration of a definite reaction; it may be favourable or decidedly adverse, but on no account should it be denied, concealed from ourself, or become the source of inner guilt. All real relationships are primarily psychic, and the psychic charge that infuses us informs us not only about the psychological and spiritual well-being of the other person, but also our sensitivity to his needs and our capacity and willingness to be of assistance to him. The third word in relationships is *vulnerability*, the capacity to receive the burden of another person's temperament and suffer under it. This occurs especially when the response to that person is adverse. It has to be borne with fortitude and as much charity as we can muster. The encounter may be destined to terminate at this point, as part of a casual social event. On the other hand, it may continue indefinitely in the setting of a family unit or an employment situation. Here it has to work itself out relentlessly.

It is in conflict rather than ethereal harmony that the character grows. We have to learn not only to tolerate people whose style of life and set of values are quite different from our own, but also to listen to what they are saying to us. This does not mean blinding ourselves to the differences or trying to plaster them over simply by finding points of common concern. It means being more firmly rooted in oneself than ever before and testing one's own previously held views and attitudes in the refining fire of another person's presence, one that appears inimicable and immediately threatening. A confrontation with a hostile witness brings us close to the unstable equilibrium within ourselves in which we balance precariously between a structured conformity to the society around us on the one hand and a destructive anarchy that would break loose from all the restraints it puts around us on the other. Every new encounter is a potential threat to our inner security, and every relationship reveals some imbalance within us.

Far from being unfortunate, this is the way of personal growth into something of a mature human being. But attention and humility are essential in the process. In this respect, humility does not mean self-denigration or a belittling of one's own unique essence. This is more akin to humiliation, unpleasant when it is visited upon us as a result of some misdemeanour which has been discovered and publicised, but perversely enjoyable when we ourselves are the agents of the flagellation. It is the reverse side of narcissistic self-approval, and in both the ego is dominant. Both have subtle sexual overtones also. Humility is simply a state of openness, being aware that we do not know much and that enlightenment can reach us from even the most improbable sources. Humility is a quality of youth; as long as one can learn from all the changes of life, one will never grow old in spirit. And the life beyond death will be the source of endless delight as one approaches its welcoming light at the end of a well-spent life on earth.

I doubt whether many friendships that have stood the test of time have escaped periods of severe conflict, so that each party has had to acknowledge considerable areas of difference, even apparent incompatibility. A relationship that requires a sedulous plastering over of the cracks of disagreement is in fact unreal. A relationship that is of real substance is progressive; it shows the essential quality of a living organism, which is growth. When one ceases to grow, death is approaching – and this is right, because it means that a particular phase of existence has been spent and something new has to take its place. A real relationship is not simply an elaborate supporting edifice where one can conceal uncongenial aspects of one's character so as to appear superficially urbane and acceptable to the other person. Such a relationship is radically unsound because it depends on mutual connivance rather than truth. The truth of friendship is support even to the point of death. A makeshift relationship that masquerades as friendship will founder on the rocks of egoistical manipulation when the outer circumstances are no longer easy and a multitude of things go wrong.

We cannot use people with impunity. For a long time an adequate modus vivendi may appear to be struck, but in due course the inner core of identity that we call the soul of the one who is manipulated will rise in revolt and cry out, as Moses did, 'Let my people go in order to worship our God' (Exod. 8:1). At that point the attachment will be revealed in all its shallowness. Not all predatory relationships are so blatantly parasitic as this; some such relationships may be so intense that they delude the protagonist into believing that he is full of love, while in other relationships love may appear to be given to as many people as possible. I refer here to infatuation on the one hand and sexual promiscuity on the other.

The person who is infatuated projects his identity on to the object of his attraction. He invades the psychic presence as well as the physical privacy of the other person. He is grasping, admittedly unconsciously, for a quality in that individual that he himself lacks, but which he sees brilliantly represented in the object of attention. His ultimate, though unconscious, aim is to gain control of that person and suck him dry of the desired qualities. This is a most terrible example of parasitism, and its end is the subtle destruction of the victim as he is drawn covetously into the personality of the predator. And yet the state of emotional gluttony and psychic invasion can mimic ardent affection so closely that the one who is possessed, as if by an outside influence, sincerely believes that he loves his victim most passionately. Love admittedly covers a multitude of sins, but it must be distinguished categorically from the morbid attachment that underlies infatuation. Love bestows the freedom to be oneself that is essential in any living relationship. The predator remains unfilled in his infatuation, whereas the lover is full of God's Spirit.

Promiscuity in relationships involves the most intimate and holy moment of dedication, sexual union. This is indeed a sacrament of God's love for us; in the act, when consummated in love, each gives of the self to the other. The cloud of forgetting, at least for a split second, descends over the clamant demands and yearnings of the personality, while the cloud of unknowing cleaves sufficiently for the light of God to be momentarily revealed. Sexual union has many benefits, but its supreme gift is the knowledge of God's love, as it breaks through the usual opacity of the personality and radiates to the depths where the spirit lies revealed. Indeed, in the words of Psalm 42 (v. 7), deep calls to deep in the roar of God's cataracts. In other words, loving sexual intercourse is the way in which the common man, who makes no claims to spiritual knowledge or aspiration, can also find release from the limitations of ego consciousness and experience mystical union with the infinite. That this is not merely a delightful, though evanescent, escape from the stress of exigent living is proved by the aura of love that surrounds the person for some time after the peak of self-transcendence. As soon as we can forget ourselves in a wider opening of our whole being to life, we begin to live with the abundance that Jesus came to show us. He did this, not only by His teaching but also, and much more relevantly, by making Himself completely available to us as He gave up His mortal life on the cross of our affliction.

But not all sexual intercourse is motivated by self-giving love. Much of it is an expression of lust, the desire for satisfaction even at the expense of another person's well-being. Sexual activity can as easily be an expression of hatred as of love. The horror of a sexual assault implants itself deeply in the psyche of the victim, because an essence of sanctity that surrounds the soul is violated, and can never be completely restored. The inner effect of rapacious sexual activity cannot be gauged simply by the outer manifestations that are evoked; a sickness of the soul persists, so that the beautiful self-giving that is at the heart of all true relationships, whether intimately genital or warmly social, may be inhibited or even completely thwarted. Only a prolonged counselling or psychotherapeutic process with deep understanding and warm affection flowing from the counsellor can repair, at least to some extent, the terrible hurt that has been done.

Of course, promiscuity in sexual relationships does not have this baneful effect, because there is at least mutual compliance in the act. But any act of genital union involves a profound psychic exchange. The one who is promiscuous can implant the psychic impression with facility, as he trails off to his next contact – and here men are considerably less vulnerable than are women. But the receptive, caring partner is left with the psychic emanation, which is much less easily dismissed from consciousness. It persists as a pervading awareness, almost an aroma, that brings unease and disquiet in its wake. Instead of love, all that remains is a subjective counterfeit, and a progressive loneliness rears its head. This is intolerable to confront, and therefore the attention is rapidly diverted to other sources of entertainment and self-comfort. The fruits of sexual promiscuity are a dulling of the individual sensitivity, a lowering of the sights of personal endeavour and integrity, and a slow regression to a coarse animal lust which eventually becomes an abiding passion of life. When the human becomes an animal, he becomes a vile beast, because he brings with him his native intelligence while lacking the natural innocence and simplicity of his animal brethren.

At his best, man is a spiritual being, at his basest a destructive beast. Sexual intercourse, of all human activities, illustrates this vast polarity and range of responses. It also shows the supreme importance of intimate human relationships in leading man from the dark inheritance of his past to the glorious light of God's radiance in the present moment which is also the portal to the future. The fruit of our ignorance about the all-pervading psychic emanation deriving from deep personal relationships and the pain that their casual disruption can produce is a trivial view and permissive attitude towards sexual conduct. This is even more the case nowadays since techniques of contraception have apparently reached a peak of efficiency. It seems a rational conclusion to encourage sexual experimentation as a sensible prelude to a more lasting union. While all relationships have an experimental aspect, and the sequence of trial and error must inevitably punctuate life's many ventures, it is nevertheless certain that sexual relationships should be initiated only in the environment of deep mutual concern. The Hindu ideal of harmlessness is perhaps the most practical approach to this difficult problem; if we could take it to heart at the start of each new undertaking we might begin to think responsibly about the probable results of our actions, and be guided accordingly.

Love comes more slowly, being indeed the measure of the

spiritually mature person. It embraces both harmlessness and self-giving. It must be acknowledged that many experimental relationships are destined to fail, but if they have been undertaken in a spirit of responsibility and respect, though their fruits may first be bitter, they will later be sweetened by the balm of understanding. There is, in other words, a middle way between taking care at all costs to keep oneself clean and uncontaminated from the world and acting with promiscuous irresponsibility so as to defile as many people as possible for one's own pleasure. The way of obsessional purity precludes any real relationship, whereas the path of promiscuity lowers human ties to animal encounters. The ultimate way is to be open in love to as many people as possible and feed them with the Holy Spirit that infuses the dedicated psyche. By this means they may be freed from over-dependence on physical comfort and genital pleasure, which by its nature cannot be other than transient, and helped to participate in spiritual fellowship, which is of unfailing support. This was the way of Jesus in His frequent encounters with the fallen members of the society of His time, and it is our paradigm of fulfilled counselling in this treacherous terrain.

Jesus never condemned the degraded members of society; on the contrary He dined with them and enjoyed their company, because they were open in their dispositions and could communicate. But He did not lower Himself to their standard in order to accommodate them; instead He raised them up to what God intended them to be. This He did by His very presence and what radiated from Him. We may be sure He did not preach repentance, as did St John the Baptist in his preparatory work, but rather flowed out in loving acceptance. This love that suffers the pain of humanity and is vulnerable to the point of death can alone bring the unlovely into fellowship with the world of value and aspiration.

And then comes the miracle: the unloved, and therefore unlovely, become infinitely lovable as they cast off their cloak of indifference and begin to make their own journey to spiritual fulfilment. They do not lose contact with their own identity; far from losing it, they encounter it fully for the first time in their lives. The venal tax-gatherer, for instance, need not wash his hands completely of all financial dealing – after all, money is also one of God's gifts to us – but now he can use his resources with wisdom and charity. They cease to be the measure of his own fulfilment as a person, and can instead be used to assist less fortunate people. In a similar fashion, the prostitute need no longer yield her body to the lustful embrace of the unfulfilled man for the sake of security. Instead, as a redeemed person, she can give of herself in her entirety, and freely too, in love to those who have never been acknowledged as persons worthy of respect, let alone affection. Her own life mirrored this lack of love that she had inherited from a loveless generation that conceived her – for the sins of the fathers are visited on their children up to the third and fourth generation (Exod. 20:5), a statement incidentally not of God's terrible wrath, but of the inevitable law of cause and effect without the redemption wrought by undemanding, self-giving love such as Christ came to show us. The reward of the redeemed prostitute is not to be measured any longer in financial terms; it is the simple joy of acknowledging another human being without any personal desire other than to watch over a vulnerable soul emerging from behind the dark barriers of a previously recalcitrant personality, from the cocoon of fear to the open warmth of love.

The psychological mechanism of sublimation of unful-filled potentialities that is so well described in psycho-analytic theory is now raised to a higher level of service and commitment by the spiritual glory of transfiguration. Psychological understanding can help a person make the most of his present endowments, however poor they may be. Spiritual wisdom can extend this basic, but very important, work by evoking an openness to the creative power of life in the love that comes from the constant, yet unobtrusive, solicitude of the counsellor. This 'creative power of life' is, incidentally, as satisfactory a definition of the work of the Holy Spirit as many humanistic agnostics would allow. But just as the common people who heard Jesus gladly were unknowingly encountering the very voice of God in whom until then they had only been able to believe from afar, so the agnostic client who is brought into direct relationship with the accepting love of a counsellor may begin to recognise the love of God by direct mystical insight. In the end all true love is known mystically, by which I mean that such love shows itself by lifting the beloved far beyond the limitations of his human nature to an apprehension of the glory of eternal union with the divine. Love, in other words, brings out the divinity lying at the core of our inner existence; it lets the spirit of the soul shine through the personality and be concentrated at the point of the ego, usually so demanding and predatory, so that Christ can show Himself in the life of the beloved, no matter how brief this appearance may be. But then one can say with the blind man whom Jesus healed, 'All I know is this: once I was blind, now I can see' (John 9:25).

It must also be acknowledged that the vast procession of human beings that we, as one of their number, encounter in a life's work, comprise a motley throng of individuals. Each is on his own rung of the ladder of spiritual development. What is right for the needs of one person in terms of relationships may not be appropriate for someone else. Furthermore, all life is growth. The opinions we held when we were young should have been considerably modified and broadened by the experience of life, and our lives on this earth are yet to be completed. Healing and growth are so complementary one to another as to be almost interchangeable categories. This is another reason why we must never judge, let alone condemn the life-style of another person. But when that life-style brings with it the exploitation or abuse of someone else, we are impelled to open the shutters of his mind so that he can begin to see the implications of his actions. The law is plain: whatever measure you deal out to others will be dealt back to you (Matt. 7:2). This terrible, though inevitable, law is fortunately subject to the other great law of forgiveness that permeates the universe and was, as Christians would assert, manifested crucially in the life of Christ. The love of God modifies and redirects the justice of God, but we have to make the first move, and this is the confession of sins. We are told elsewhere in the Sermon on the Mount 'Ask, and you will receive; seek, and you will find; knock, and the door will be opened. For everyone who asks receives, he who seeks finds, and to him who knocks, the door will be opened' (Matt. 7:7–8). But we have to seek, to ask and finally to knock at the door of the soul, so that He who knocks patiently at the other side, awaiting admission, may be allowed in to sit down to supper with us and we with Him (Rev. 3:20).

Counselling therefore has two aspects; the love of acceptance and the stern direction of the Holy Spirit leading the client on his way, divested of all illusions and disembarrassed of all unnecessary possessions, to become a person in his own right.

12.

The Need to be Wanted

We share a common need, that of love. We need to be acknowledged and wanted, to be of use and esteemed for ourselves alone. Conversely, we all share a basic insecurity, that in essence we do not really matter at all, that our contribution counts for nothing, that the world could get on well enough without us, that, if we were to disappear even for a short time, we should be neither missed nor lamented, and that our absence would pass to total oblivion in the memories of those among whom we once worked and played our part.

We have already seen that St Augustine diagnosed the human condition as one of restlessness until the soul rests in God, Who made mankind for Himself alone. The natural mystic is not far from the knowledge of God, but most people grope ineffectively for the divine presence throughout their lives even if they are loyal members of a worshipping community. We might believe that to know God is to be eternally nourished by His presence and comforted by His embrace so that our journey in life is virtually over even before it has really begun. But even this is questionable. God may want us for Himself alone, but He demands that we bring our fellow creatures with us to Him. Life is not a simple communion between God and the individual; it comprises a trinity of God, the individual and the community.

The natural mystic, through his very closeness to the divine essence, feels his great separation from the multitudes around him. This separation does not engender an attitude of spiritual superiority, as in the Parable of the Publican and the Pharisee, where, it may be remembered, the self-righteous Pharisee thanked God that he was so unlike other men, for instance, the despicable tax-gatherer beside him in the Temple (Luke 18:9–14). The separation that spiritual sensitivity brings with it makes the mystic yearn for human solidarity and fellowship. Jesus says 'Foxes have their holes, the birds their roosts; but the Son of Man has nowhere to lay his head' (Matt. 8:20). This statement does not emphasise the material hardships of the spiritual life so much as its emotional isolation. To lay one's head in tranquil sleep after a heavy day's work requires an environment of trust and caring even more than a comfortable bed and decent lodgings. The natural mystic has difficulty with the language of mundane aspiration; he cannot thrill to the desires of the common man, for his head is up in the cloud of unknowing where God's presence lies concealed. Nevertheless, he has to master the vernacular also, just as Christ did at the moment of His incarnation and especially when He was baptised and led out into the human wilderness by the Holy Spirit to experience the full range of temptation prepared by the forces of evil that rule the distraught passions of unredeemed men.

It may be thought that all the giving comes from the mystic, as from Christ, who though rich, for our sake became poor, so that through His poverty we might become rich (2 Cor. 8:9). But in fact the mystic increases in spiritual stature as he gains other insights into holiness from the common man. He has to come to understand the spirituality of sweat and toil, of self-sacrifice on behalf of his family, of hope in the face of obviously impending failure. Christ himself, though the pre-existent Son of God, grew into an even greater glory than before through His time in the world with us as a man among men. Though innocent of sin, yet for our sake God made Him one with the sinfulness of men, so that in Him we might be made one with the goodness of God Himself (2 Cor. 5:21). The full mystery of the Incarnation is beyond rational analysis just as the Atonement wrought by the suffering and death of Christ is something that becomes increasingly lucid only as the life of enforced renunciation is followed in trust and fortitude. But if the one on the path can be supported by a counsellor who knows something of the way, his progress can be greatly facilitated. In the end he too will enter the ranks of those who understand and therefore can be of help to his fellows.

It appears therefore that the spiritually gifted person has to learn the parlance of everyday life in order to do the work set out for him. On the other hand, the common man has to attain a knowledge of things eternal so that his personal concerns may be extended to communal, and ultimately universal, service. It is in self-giving service that freedom can alone be known. The work, those served and the One Who provides, namely God, take over the life of the servant, who loses himself progressively as he attains a true selfhood in God. This is indeed the way of the mystic reduced to a simple formula, and it is my belief that we are all called on to know something of the mystical path, the path of direct apprehension of God, even though in any one generation only a few seem to be consciously on the way. Jesus says 'The gate that leads to life is small and the road is narrow, and those who find it are few' (Mat. 7:14). The work of the counsellor is to direct the client on to that road and encourage him on a way that is hard because of its loneliness, but is itself the ultimate reward in each step taken. He is the way, the truth and the life (John 14:6) – not merely the destination but each step on the way. We know Him even now when we lose self in service, and in the end we shall know Him in our brother and in every aspect of the world around us. This means that the true counsellor must also be on the road.

One of the revealing aspects of spiritual counselling is that each step of the way is concealed until we make the inward movement in faith. In the adventure of life we all share a common ignorance, unlike some rather assured protagonists of the various schools of psychodynamic theory who can place people summarily in various predetermined categories. They often seem to know the problem even before it is fully enunciated and to have the right answer already prepared. But in fact there is seldom a completely right answer to any human problem. Often one special area of difficulty may stand out so clearly that it obviously needs immediate attention, but underneath there are sure to be many other factors that may also need investigation and healing. The cloud of unknowing leads to the kingdom of heaven where healing is consummated in self-giving love to the neighbour who becomes oneself also. For when we love our neighbour as ourself, the barriers that separate us drop and we see ourselves in the other person. This is a precious fruit of mystical illumination in practical living.

The need to be wanted is the outward assertion of our inner identity. Identity is itself somewhat pallid and unformed until it asserts itself, proclaiming its existence and its need for manifesting itself among its peers in the world. The infant cries to bring itself and its needs to the attention of its parents and attendants. The unloved child will resort to exhibitionistic gestures and even criminal activity to the same end, while the unacknowledged adult may show a range of bizarre behaviour patterns to make himself heard and heeded. These patterns may extend from anti-social actions on the one hand to hysterical outbursts and physical ill-health on the other. To be acknowledged as a person we need *caring relationships*, *work* to afford material sustenance and also to provide us with a basis of self-esteem and an interest in the wider world, and *a well-disposed society* as a member of which we can play our part in the flow of life around us. Thus we are acknowledged firstly by those close to us in love, secondly by our working companions, and finally by those kindred spirits who share our private interests in such social fields as sport, the arts, politics or philanthropic endeavour. A well-balanced life should be fairly equally poised on this threefold support. As we grow older our dependence on employment declines, whereas relationships form an even more essential basis of meaning in our life than they did previously. The character of our friends and associates sheds much light on the quality of our own identity, whether it is warm and elevating or cold and grimy.

The three needs to be satisfied for our own identity to be firmly established are, to repeat them once again, *personal love, a fulfilling livelihood* and *creative participation in the wider community.* How does one acquire these and work towards their maintenance and growth, remembering that anything ceasing to grow starts to die? We have already considered the deep springs of love. Though love is of God, we too have to play our part by developing our capacity to receive it, contain it, and give it to those around us. In other words, God provides love, but it is our work to use it and distribute it to those around us. By prayer even those far off, whom we have never met personally, may gain love from us. The wonder of spiritual attainments is that they endow the agent with ever more proficiency and power; the gifts he bestows on others are returned to him, renewed in spiritual power and illuminated in wisdom. As Jesus said, 'Give, and gifts will be given you. Good measure, pressed down, shaken together, and running over, will be poured into your lap' (Luke 6:38).

The type of person who has difficulty with relationships has to be taught to look inward to his own deficiencies. When one misfortune follows another, whether it is ill-health, a breakdown in family relationships, an accident, or some shattering blow whether in love or in one's career, one is being told to examine one's own life and its priorities carefully. One will never receive constant affection until one has learned to bestow at least some measure of concern on another person. Some problems of relationships, as we have already noted elsewhere, are due to the poor opinion the person has of himself; the ego-structure can be blighted if one is denied proper acknowledgment, acceptance and love early in one's life by virtue of an uncaring, if not hostile, family background. It must also be said though that some of the most remarkable people it has been my privilege to know have come from such appalling backgrounds that psychological and sociological theory would have condemned them summarily to delinquency and irreversible emotional breakdown. Instead they have shown me the way of love and sanctity.

There is another type of person who has a strong awareness of his ego, but requires a constant flow of stimuli to satisfy it. He flits from one thing to another, floats from one person to another, sullying everything he touches and bringing no creative impulse to any work he may perform or any relationship he may initiate. His promiscuity is not so much malicious and predatory as instinctive and insensitive. When his numerous ventures collapse – whether these be business undertakings or personal relationships – he feels let down and disillusioned. If he has tried to stabilise a sexual relationship by marriage, this too disintegrates and adds its tale to the horrifying statistics of marital breakdown. He seems to have no difficulty in initiating new ventures, but lacks the staying power, the constancy, to maintain them. With the advent of years, he has to face the threat of a lonely, unfulfilled middle and later life. The circumstance that often brings such a person – no less tragic than the Prodigal Son – to himself is some catastrophe. This may be a serious illness, the death of someone who meant more to him than he would previously have admitted, or the collapse of some professional or business venture which had been the mainstay of his life. The growing menace of redundancy adds greater bite to this threat of personal annihilation.

Such a calamity tears the false image away from the previously heedless person, so that, for the first time in his life, he can see himself clearly. And what is seen is stark and terrifying: a focus of enfeeblement surrounded by the dark threat of non-existence. One way out of this terrible vision of imprisonment and impenetrable hopelessness is suicide, but an intuitive understanding will show the person that such a course of action would serve to perpetuate the condition rather than end it. But if he can be still like the Prodigal Son, the voice of God will address him incontestably from the hidden depths of his own soul, and he will be led back to life and the people he had misused, now, however, in abject humility. To confess one's sins to God is to be forgiven provided the will is dedicated to making an honest new start. The counsellor acts as an intermediary, almost an intercessor, in this act of repentance, and he is the means by which a new directive of living can be addressed to the benumbed client. As soon as the emptiness of the shriven, cleansed soul is filled with the divine presence, love enters the life of the penitent and the way of service can be broached. Paradoxically, this service will be the first taste of freedom, the first inner liberty, the person has experienced in his life. In due course that freedom will be fertilised and fulfilled by many relationships of outflowing warmth. These will no longer depend on the pleasure derived from the other person but on mutual respect and service offered and later by the intensity of the love that flows between them. Furthermore, this is merely the prelude to the love that will circulate among many other souls on the path of life.

When there is no dramatic event to point incontrovertibly to the person's selfish, heedless past, but only a series of unsatisfactory relationships that seem always to end on a muted note of futility and gathering hopelessness, that person's own life must be probed and his motives analysed. The work of self-analysis is facilitated by the crisp contributions made by the counsellor, but the action must be undertaken by the client himself. As he begins to acknowledge the superficiality of his relationships with others and the perfunctory use he made of their emotional vulnerability to gain control over them, so he has to face the spectre of his own dark sinfulness. Once again a candid admission of guilt confirmed by a vow to live a very different type of life in the future guarantees forgiveness. Then a new life of service is born where previously there was only selfishness and lust.

The important spiritual law of healing, whether on the level of counselling or on a more obviously charismatic basis, is that no person can heal us, whether that person is some marvellously gifted minister of healing or simply ourselves. The same applies to the more orthodox channels of medical care and psychotherapy. God alone is the healer, but all the agents of healing can help to put the patient in the best situation for the healing energies of the Holy Spirit to do their reparative work. This truth about our own impotence, except in unstinted co-operation with God, to effect either our own healing or that of anyone else, is a fundamental Christian insight. We are justified, or brought into right relationship with God, by faith and not by our own merits and calculated works, and it is the same faith that leads us to a full encounter with the healing power of the Holy Spirit.

The very fact that we cannot heal ourselves is a source of infinitely great relief, for otherwise our growing feeling of guilt at continued ill-health would be unbearable. But if we are still and trusting and our will is dedicated to a new life of service, healing will come to us, either apparently directly from God, or more probably through the mediation of some minister of healing, of which the counsellor is a central representative. This applies especially to the work of counselling, for even if the 'thorn in the flesh' is not to be taken away, as in the case of St Paul, we will be given a double measure of supernatural strength to cope with the difficulty by rising to an unaccustomed height of endeavour and spiritual freedom. God's power not infrequently comes to its full strength in weakness, since His grace is all we need (2 Cor. 12:9).

Our need for personal love is the central theme of life. How many people do we not all know who, despite their considerable talents in everyday living and even their great intellectual or artistic gifts, feel inveterate outsiders in the arena of life! They long for acknowledgment, to be told that they really do matter in their society and that they would be genuinely missed if they were to depart. Many such people hold responsible positions in their particular professions or skills, and many are apparently suitably married and with families of their own. But they simply cannot relate on a deep level to anyone despite the fact that they themselves have unexplored depths to their own personalities. If they were shallow people, their contact with their families would cease quite spontaneously and satisfactorily at the level of genital sexuality on the one hand and mutual support in material matters on the other. But they are sufficiently aware of the great issues of existence – of life and death – to know that inner fulfilment is to be found only at greater depths than these. They are, in fact, longing for God, in Whom alone their restless souls can find peace, but they will not know Him until they know themselves in self-abandoned love for a fellow human being – and ultimately a large number of human beings. In Christ this love is universal, and we are all destined to become Christs, to partake fully of the divine nature, to come to share in the very being of God (2 Pet. 1:4).

To attain personal love we must first of all cease striving for it. Love cannot be grasped. Any predatory action has the immediate effect of lifting love out of our grasp, so that all that is left to us is the illusion of caring that evaporates like an early morning mist. Love is delicate and vulnerable, self-effacing and shy. It comes quietly to us when we are quiet and undemanding, but evades our importunate cry when we are obsessed with its necessity in our lives. It is the great privilege of the counsellor to give the yearning soul of his client its first taste of real love, to make the person feel that he really does count for something in the world, and that at least one other person does care for him and look forward to his visit. The great work of the counsellor is to flow out in love, a love of acceptance garnished with wisdom. This love is not the same as affection; it is altogether deeper and more constant. Affection is also a beautiful quality, but it depends on one's temperament and one's capacity to flow out in gestures of warm welcome to other people. Affection can easily be aroused, and it soon can become an automatic response to any appealing newcomer. To the one who is less attractive the flow of affection soon dries up and is succeeded by subtle aversion that cannot so easily be masked. The value of gestures of affection is that they break down barriers of reserve and diffidence, but if they are not accompanied by a deeper caring, they are as likely to lead to seduction as to a flowering of the personality of the one to whom they are directed.

Love, on the other hand, is calm, constant, undiscriminating and penetrating. It may be accompanied by gestures of affection, such as kissing and embraces, but in its depth it is silent, concentrated and undemonstrative. But it will never relinquish the other person, for, as St Paul writes, 'Love will never come to an end' (1 Cor. 13:8). This unfailing quality is the criterion of love. Even if the beloved fails miserably, the lover bears with him in prayer even if direct contact may, for one reason or another, have to be discontinued for the time being. To be able to flow out in constant love is the prerequisite of effective counselling. Since love is of God and we love because He loved us first (I John 4:19), the counsellor must be in a state of inner contemplation with God as he flows out in love to his client. This love is not sentimental or effusive; it is cool, deliberate and wise. It does not seek to ingratiate itself, but to heal that which is broken, to bring into proper alignment that which is crooked and perverse, to restore sight to that which is blind, and to infuse new life into the disconsolate soul of the despairing person. Love will never let the other person down even if it is severely disappointed at his poor showing. If, for instance, one who loved us heard unpleasant reports about our private life, his intuitive response would be to disregard them and to defend our reputation against the calumny of our detractors. Even if this report proved in fact to be an accurate assessment of the situation, his love would flow out to support us in the trial of our humiliation. It would know that this present aberration was not the quintessence of our personality or even a summary of its main trends; on the contrary, it would see the truth of Christ enshrined in its deepest recess, which is the spirit. St Paul says, 'There is nothing love cannot face; there is no limit to its faith, its hope and its endurance (1 Cor. 13:7). This is the love which must infuse the counsellor in all his relationships, not only the professional ones, but also those of his private life.

There cannot be two classes of loving: the simulated concern for the client and the all too obvious insensitivity to those with whom we live and work day by day. Likewise true religion is not relegated to Sabbath observance only, but to every moment of our life in eternity. As Jesus points out, 'The Sabbath was made for the sake of man and not man for the Sabbath' (Mark 2:27). The object of the discipline of prayer is to put us into such perfect silent relationship with

God that we may carry that heavenly peace with us as we pursue our daily work in a world that is neither heavenly nor peaceful. Our presence should bring God's peace to whatever situation He has called us to witness and to whomsoever He has directed us to serve. For His is the spirit of healing while we are His agents. When we are open in love to God and our fellow men, His divine wisdom enters our heart and mind, and the words spoken are of timeless import and priceless value. It is then that the treasury of the Bible becomes fully available to us, and we can say, in a spirit of illumination, that scripture is indeed God's word spoken through inspired prophets and sages. Truth, in other words, is timeless: Jesus Christ is the same yesterday, today and for ever (Heb. 13:8). This is in essence the nature of the spirit of counsel.

Therefore, when a person needs desperately to be wanted, he must first of all be accepted and welcomed by the counsellor. His story, common as it may be on one level, is a unique document of a soul's stumbling progress in a life of trial and triumph. As we listen, so the spark of God's compassion radiates from us as warmth, caring, concern and, finally, love. Once the person has experienced this love that will never betray or relinquish him, he must be taught the secret of love, which is availability to God's grace at all times and in all situations. Only as we can bestow love do we ourselves become more and more wanted by others. The steps in learning how to love are as follows: first, silent meditation on the course of one's own life, followed by a confession to God (through the mediation, if need be, of the counsellor) of one's past insensitivity, cruelty and selfishness in whatever relationships one may have had. Then comes the silence in which God can begin to heal both the memories and the resentments, while restoring one's image of oneself to something of the quality of Christ Himself. The end of this inner renewal is a return to the world in peace, with a willed intent to serve others in love for the remainder of one's life. There are two supports in this resolve: God's unfailing presence that can be approached at any time in prayer, and His representative here on earth, the counsellor. The process, as outlined, seems childishly simple and its results extremely rapid. In fact, it will occupy the remainder of the person's life as well as that of the counsellor, for 'love is patient; love is kind and envies no one' (1 Cor. 13:4). Constancy characterises the devoted counsellor, and even when the client has moved effectively into his own private life and no longer needs the counsellor – a movement always to be encouraged – the link of prayer will bind both to God in the upward movement of both souls to the eternal knowledge of love.

13.

The Identity Crisis

We have seen that the realisation of our unique identity as an individual in the society around us balances precariously on the three prongs of caring relationships, a fulfilling livelihood, and an ability to participate creatively in the life of the wider community by means of hobbies and various social activities. The importance of the second of these, a satisfactory occupation, in establishing a healthy self-esteem, can hardly be over-emphasised. One's image of oneself is built up in no small measure in terms of one's daily work.

In the recesses of the mind, half conscious and half unconscious, there is often to be found an exalted personage, based usually on a real person who meant much to us when we were very young. It remains a constant companion, both comforting and critical, standing in judgment over us and the conduct of our lives. Whatever we do and say is calculated to impress this figure who provides us with a standard of inner approval. This censorious figure is, of course, an element of the Freudian superego, and its sex is determined by that of the real person who provided the psychic material for its construction many years previously. It may in some instances represent the dominating figure in the superego, which is of immediate relevance in one's life. Alternatively, it may act as a symbol for the entire superego in its most approachable form. Here it is almost tangible physically while being fully available emotionally. A life-size artefact can be of comfort to us when we are lonely and feel alienated from the society around us, but it eventually tends to assume a dominating role that impedes the free development of the personality. The reason for this interference is that it irrupts into the focus of our true identity, so that we tend to see ourselves in terms of this superego figure instead of our true individuality. When life is going smoothly for us and the auguries are favourable, the figure can be dealt with summarily and put in its place; but when all is awry, the figure assumes a judgmental role. It seems to reproach one for one's own inadequacy and taunt one with one's failures. The figure has to be expunged, indeed exorcised, from the psyche. Paradoxically, this cleansing function may be achieved by an identity crisis which seems to cut away the very ground from under one's feet.

It is important to distinguish between a crisis in identity and a basic failure to establish a viable ego awareness. The identity crisis occurs as a dramatic event in which there is a tearing down of what appeared to be a stable identity with its imposing outer façade, the image we show to the world. By contrast, a failure in basic ego-structure is with one from one's conception; it is carried along as a constant incubus until one grows in self-esteem. The person in an identity crisis suddenly finds himself bereft of the identity he once assumed was his own; it is as if his shadow or his reflection were subtly stolen from him and his inner substance emptied out and dematerialised so that a hollow shell is all that is left. He becomes a wraith-like figure, like the inhabitants of the Old Testament place of the dead, Sheol, who were insubstantial ghosts devoid of any of the properties of living creatures. This shattering of one's old way of life, that one so took for granted and on which one's identity rested so firmly and proudly, can follow a number of unheralded events of disastrous consequence: an especially topical one is redundancy from work at an age considerably below that of customary retirement. The breaking up of a long-established friendship due to betrayal is another event that may empty one's life of something that was previously its mainstay. And then there is the tragedy of bereavement. To this list there must also be added the inroads of bodily disease and dysfunction of the special senses that put an end to many previously held presuppositions about one's place in the world and the future ahead of one. The pleasant experiences of life serve to round out our personalities, but growth follows hardship. The rounding-out process is like a cosy Sunday afternoon's nap after a heavy lunch – it is enjoyable, but its aftermath is slightly depressing. It contains within it a vague presage of the passage of time bringing with it an aura of disintegration and death. Growth is vigorous, like a solitary walk through the bare fields on a cold winter's morning. It is indeed a journey through death on towards the new life ahead. 'No one who sets his hand to the plough and then keeps looking back is fit for the kingdom of God' (Luke 9:62).

The greatest privilege of responsible adult life is having a rewarding occupation. The reward is not merely a financial one; much more significant is the confirming, substantiating effect that employment has on the ego. It makes one feel of importance in one's social milieu by virtue of what one achieves, and it also eases one's attention off one's own immediate problems by focusing it on to an outer, manageable interest. Admittedly to many people work is simply an unending drudgery made acceptable only by the periods of rest and recreation that punctuate it. Little do they realise that if the work were suddenly removed and all their life could be spent, if they so willed it, in an atmosphere of relaxation or on a never-ending holiday, a terrible hiatus would open out menacingly in front of them. When one's employment suddenly comes to an end, one is brought face to face with a meaningless existence in which one colourless day succeeds another. Even if every comfort is laid on, one is enveloped by a terrible boredom so that eventually one may yearn, however shamefacedly, for something to happen, even a disaster if need be, that might shatter the cold, barren monotony that embraces one like a funeral shroud. People who are wealthy enough not to need to earn a living soon come to detest the gilded prison that money can provide, and the more enterprising lose no time in breaking free by engaging in constructive work. Money is a very equivocal aid to personal fulfilment: its absence can leave one miserable, but its presence even to excess seldom brings happiness with it. The investment of his riches can provide a diversion for the wealthy man, but it does not help him to grow into a full person. On the contrary, this way of life can help him to evade the great issues of existence, to the extent of being effectively barred from entering the kingdom of heaven. To enter here we have to bring ourselves alone, naked of all guile. The presence of wealth in whatever form prevents our entry. The path that leads to eternal life is narrow to the point of accommodating the person on it alone. All else has to be left behind.

At one time the call was for work that fulfilled one as a person. Nowadays the need is even more basic: to have something to do. The unemployment that follows enforced redundancy threatens the lives of millions of people. The moral threat it presents to the young is itself a terrifying spectre of the wrath to come. The disillusionment and desolation that face many who have given years of their lives to their work is a human tragedy. Where the social services are adequate, at least the basic requirements for respectable living can be maintained – food, clothing and housing. But the aspect of poverty that is not so easily counteracted is the silent humiliation of the personality faced with rejection. The person without employment, ceasing to play his part in the world's round of work, lies like a discarded piece of débris on a scrap-heap of public apathy and private despair. His self-respect has taken a severe beating; in terms of his use to society and the expectation of his own future life, he feels he might as well be dead. The tragedy of unemployment brings one to a direct encounter with the springs of one's integrity. In the end, if we are to survive this up-rooting of our assumed, illusory identity together with the painful scrutiny of the superego that sustained it, we have to grow into a very different person. This is in fact a variation on a cosmic theme; without the experience of crucifixion there can be no real understanding of resurrection.

Our identity is a joyous awareness of our own significance in the scheme of life. It is at its peak when we can take it for granted and accept it unconditionally. It seems especially strong when we are anchored firmly to some occupational or professional role. This role determines our life-style, giving us a secure place in the society to which we belong. It decrees with a splendid precision the routine of our life from the time of rising in the morning to retiring at night. Our role in society is what we believe we are. For a long time we may be able to maintain this façade of identity; while a mechanism moves evenly, it remains harmoniously poised within its environment.

And then comes the end; with shattering finality the work is taken away and the routine within which one lived is disrupted. Now it does not appear to matter when one arises or when one goes to bed. What one does with the day is immaterial, indeed irrelevant. Time is there to be expended; the rather terrifying expression of 'killing time' becomes meaningful with an urgent force. Time is now one's greatest enemy, and the less clamantly it reveals its relentless presence and slow passage, the more secure one feels. The attraction of drink and drugs can be almost irresistible, since they deaden, albeit temporarily, one's awareness of the present situation of futility and the future menace of depersonalisation. Entertainments have a hollow resonance since at the back of the scene lies the darkness of personal blight and an all-embracing futility of purposeless life. A drive through beautiful scenery is a glorious experience provided one has a destination to reach. It is a piquant human paradox that as one proceeds through the attractive fields and forests of the countryside, so one secretly inveighs against the speed necessary to reach one's place of call. It would be so much more desirable to spend unlimited time in these beautiful natural surroundings than to pay a visit to some friend living in a comparatively prosaic dwelling-place. The journey seems more rewarding than the destination; indeed, our expectations in life are often more enjoyable than their ultimate fulfilment, which usually has a deflating quality about it. All this is, needless to say, a juvenile, immature approach to reality, but few of us choose to grow up; adulthood on the emotional and spiritual levels is forced on us involuntarily by the vicissitudes of life.

When one has no work to do, the unreal quality of entertainment shows itself starkly and pitilessly. A drive taken simply to relieve present monotony loses its delight even when the most picturesque countryside is traversed. This applies especially to the person who is alone in his plight. The fantasy of spending endless time in a situation of natural beauty is exploded summarily when one is confronted with its realisation. The appeal of natural beauty, like any other aesthetic experience, depends on its transience. If it is with oneself as a sole companion, it soon loses its attractiveness and begins to pall rapidly. In the same way even the greatest music becomes lifeless with too frequent hearing, especially when we have little else to stimulate our interest, and we would not choose to read the same book over and over again, no matter how much we enjoyed it on first acquaintance. In this respect it is a tribute to the divine inspiration of Holy Scripture that it never ceases to fill us with the knowledge of things eternal no matter how often we read it. Its contents are so vast that they illumine the full range of deeper human experience and never fail to speak to our present condition. There is admittedly a paucity of humour in most of the world's great spiritual treasury; this seems to be given one personally by God as one moves beyond life's tragedy and enters the realm of holiness where the fool is king and a little child leads all God's creatures.

From all this it is apparent that our life is fulfilled according to the destination we seek. Once the clarity of the end-point becomes blurred, and the destination recedes, the journey assumes a threatening meaninglessness, since the place of return is simply where we started from, but without any intervening fulfilment or enlightenment. Likewise, a holiday becomes an essential part of each year's routine by taking us away from our work and allowing us to relax in different, pleasant surroundings. But when the holiday has spent itself, we are relieved and glad to return to our work once more, refreshed and renewed for the undertakings ahead of us. If there is no work, every day becomes a holiday but without the prospect of a return to creative existence. Such a perpetual holiday is rather like an epitome of hell; there is a terrible, impersonal apathy with no one available to care for the desolate soul of the newcomer. Man was made for an end, and if this is thwarted he lives in a limbo of unrelieved discontent and ill-defined menace. Where there is no progress the person moves perilously on the path of disintegration. Christ, as we have seen, is the way, the truth and the life (John 14:6). He is every step on the way, and the destination of our human existence is His full realisation in our life. In Him alone is the truth that sets us free from illusion, especially the illusion of false identity. In Him alone is the life of abundance in which we are loosed from the anchorage to a false or incomplete image of ourselves, so that we may enter fully into His identity transposed to our own naked individuality and made effective in our own personality.

All these considerations should impinge themselves on the counsellor when he is confronted by a person facing the threat of self-revelation that comes when redundancy strikes at the heart of his security. In this respect, his situation differs from that of the normally-retired person, whose sufferings are much less acute. He is older, and should have enjoyed the full thrust of his creative impulse. The combination of respectable age and a livelihood pursued diligently and profitably during the fertile seasons of active life before the autumn of retrenchment and the winter of immobilisation and decrepitude have struck, make a normal retirement not only acceptable but also comforting. Now at last one's time is one's own; the clock ceases to dominate the speed of one's activities and the hard, taxing routine of duties that determined one's daily life is now at an end. Time is at last available for one to pursue one's private interests, and a more direct part can be played in matters of social concern. In this freedom that is the fruit of a lifetime's work and service well bestowed, one can begin quite spontaneously to enjoy the vast range of nature's beauty and grandeur throughout the seasons of fecundity as well as the months of barrenness. The destination is the moment in hand, which might quite logically be the last one for the person if death were to strike a sudden, welcome blow at the gates of eternity, so that they might open to receive the newcomer. It is then that God is seen in every step of the way. But His presence is the destination also, which has at least been glimpsed and the way forward dimly revealed to the elderly person now happily retired.

Life on earth should end when we have completed the work we came here to do. The greatest work is ourselves and our place of operation is wherever we find ourselves; the tools are the means at hand. Every experience is a stepping-stone towards completion, the dark no less than the bright. Each moment is here to lead us away from self-centredness to self-dedication, a dedication to God Who at once throws us back to the people around us. The essence of divine worship is loving service to our neighbours who are seen ultimately to be all living forms. When we are somebody, we have to learn that we are nobody – the humiliation of redundancy teaches us this lesson loud and clear. When we are nobody, Christ dwells fully in us and we can start to do the work that God has appointed for us. Then at last we are properly about our Father's business.

What then is the work ahead of the person made redundant? The work is to listen to what God is telling him about his past life, his careless attitude to people and things that was a product of ease and complacency. We start to meditate on the past when its present fruits emerge, and begin to see that we played our part also in the upheaval in front of us. Had work been regarded as a joy and a privilege in the past, it is probable that the dire economic consequences of irresponsibility and apathy that confront nations no less than individuals would have been averted, or at least mitigated. Of course, these sobering thoughts cannot relieve the present distress, but they do serve to put us in the right frame of mind for coping with what lies in store for us. It was the threat of imminent death that made the Prodigal Son wake up and come to himself; he contemplated the past with shame as he saw how he had wasted his money in debauchery. Then the Holy Spirit deep within him led him on to a return home, humiliated and defeated but with a faith in the acceptance of his father, who symbolises our eternal Father. When one surveys the indiscipline and apathetic moral standards that over the last few decades seem to have undermined the entire international scene, we can scarcely marvel at their consequences in terms of human dereliction and economic crisis. God is indeed not to be fooled; as a man sows, so shall he reap the reward of his actions (Gal. 6:7–9).

The way forward for the person who has tasted the bitter

fruits of humiliation and despair is to look to the immediate present and be available to serve those in greater need than himself. Obviously he would like to return to the type of work he was forced to relinquish, but this desire is seldom likely to be granted, at least until a substantial period in the wilderness has been endured. One's self-esteem has to be grounded on something more substantial and durable than one's work and the money that it earns. Indeed, one's estimation of oneself has, at least for a time, to be swallowed up in one's concern for those around one who are less fortunate than one – the maimed, the mentally ill, the criminal and the drug addict. The end of this concern is a complete identification with the apparent failures of society. This is the moment of birth of a new identity: the life I now live is not my life, but the life which Christ lives in me (Galatians 2:19). We have quoted this insight before on more than one occasion; it is thus that the ideal grasps attainment. The way of complete identification with human life – and perhaps all life – was the way that Christ showed as He completed His ministry on earth. His last companions were two criminals nailed on either side of Him on a cross. We too have to undergo this precipitously downward journey before we can know who we are and what we should be doing with our life on earth – as a preparation for eternal life. Not everyone is destined to undergo extreme privation or terrible suffering, but each has to descend into his depths before he can raise them to God in aspiration and prayer. In fact, of course, it is the divine initiative that raises us up to Him, but we have to be completely open to His embrace, concealing nothing of ourselves. Only then can we be completely open to all conditions of men, and help to bring them also to God for healing and resurrection.

An identity crisis, whether it is precipitated by redundancy, bereavement or incapacitating illness, takes us out of our customary rut of comfort where we may protect ourselves from the outbursts of discontent and agony of the world around us. We then find that we have identified ourselves far too intimately with that rut which we may call our profession, our social position, our reputation or even our dependence on another person whom we believe we love passionately – just as Peter sincerely believed that he loved his Master, before His betrayal, sufficiently to give up his life for Him. Only when the object of our dependence, whether it is a personal quality or gift or a deep human relationship, has been taken from us can we descend to the depths and discover who we really are. As Psalm 130 says 'Out of the depths have I called to thee, O Lord; Lord hear my cry. Let thine ears be attentive to my plea for mercy'. It reminds us that but for God's forgiveness none could hold up his head, but God does forgive and therefore He is revered.

This is the moment of truth, the truth of God that sets us free from all illusions, especially that of ownership. In God alone is our safety. Nothing belongs to us in this world; at the most we are given custody over it. Our role is that of a steward, but in due course all earthly things recede from our control, and we have to move out fearlessly into the unknown. This does not mean that our custodianship was of no importance; on the contrary, if it was undertaken with serious intent it will have helped us to grow in responsibility and caring. We in turn by our concern for even the most simple object help to lift up its substance to something of eternal value. And when the object of our caring is a fellow human being, both of us rise to unprecedented heights of self-sacrifice and nobility.

In these thoughts we can begin to glimpse the meaning of the resurrection of the body that plays a central role in the Christian hope: not simply continued life, but an entry into the being of God as the perishable thing is raised imperishable. Sown in humiliation, it is raised in glory; sown in weakness, it is raised in power; sown as an animal body, it is raised as a spiritual body (1 Cor. 15:42–3). In the great work of resurrection God is supreme, but in His sublime courtesy He works through us, at least in our little world. When one phase of life has been completed, a new one opens up for us. In this way we can begin to face the consequences of a shattering of a past identity pattern which was based on the work we used to do or the relationships that we once enjoyed. As the past is cleared away, so a vista of the future opens out for us. Its essential qualities are simplicity and service rendered out of loving concern without any consideration of worldly rewards.

Two destructive attitudes that may rear their heads as part of an identity crisis are resentment and fear. The resentment that floods the mind with intense bitterness, a bitterness that rails against the premature termination of employment or the death of someone close in relationship, can be frighteningly destructive in its fury. It is exacerbated when one compares oneself with one's contemporaries who have been fortunate enough to retain their position, and one's juniors who are assiduously ascending to the ranks of power where one too once enjoyed security and the esteem of others. The fear of the future, that has a numbing, depersonalising character, is in essence a dread of annihilation, since one's life can no longer be identified and justified by some special routine of work. It is especially gripping during the small hours of the morning when all our adverse emotional responses assume gargantuan proportions and the darkness around us, spiritual no less than physical, seems impenetrable. Later on in the day our normal waking consciousness cuts the fear down to size as the rays of God's hope shine on our psyche and we are given the courage to venture on new paths of affirmation.

The counsellor can play an invaluable part in infusing hope into the desolate psyche of the person who is out of work or bereaved. While he himself has to find a new niche, the moral and spiritual support of one who cares can supply the person with the necessary impetus to move ahead with determination into the future. Work can seldom be supplied to the one in need, and indeed it is important that he should discover for himself where his true interests lie. Where there is heavy unemployment those who look for work cannot choose too fastidiously what they would be prepared to undertake. They have to be constantly open to the voice of God, to find out what His business entails. At least in the early stages, this is very likely to involve service to others. The work is not to be seen in terms of material reward so much as fulfilling a deeper need for human relationships. As we give ourselves fully in concern for other people, so the fears and resentments of the past gradually fade from our view, being supplanted by a faint glow of hope as the future unfolds. Eventually that hope may blaze forth into a new zest for living as a purpose for life shows itself. And this purpose will almost certainly be of a different order from the livelihood that was once the focus of one's identity.

The important lesson an identity crisis teaches us is that, although we are bound to make mistakes in the perilous course of mortal life, nothing is irremediable. Provided we have the humility and wisdom to sit down at our place of greatest perplexity, as did the Prodigal Son when he had to survey the fruits of his improvident life-style, the voice of God will show us how to proceed. The past is forgiven, and in addition the experience that accrued from its many misfortunes will be of great value to us in the future as we direct the remaining portion of our life on earth more profitably to our own concerns and those of our neighbours also. For as we grow in identity, so we can identify more completely with the society around us.

But there was another man who also came to himself at his place of greatest perplexity – Job the righteous. His identity was that of a sage, a philanthropist, a perfectly just man. Could any of us want a more seemly image than this? But only when this identity was apparently stripped from him by the advent of bereavement, financial disaster and a breakdown in health, did he come to himself. He saw that he was nothing when he had pleaded all the substance of his case with great eloquence in the debate with his comforters. Then there was silence. That is our true identity: the mute incomprehension of our crucifixion and the faith to say with Christ, 'It is accomplished'. Only then we are ready to receive God into our conscious life, as Job did when all the debating had ended in the stillness of ignorance. Then at last we can know our true identity – that of a son of God, in the image of God's only-begotten Son. When our weary souls find their well-sought rest in God, they become like Him, and at last our identity exceeds even that of our native society. It embraces all humanity, indeed all life. As we have lost ourselves in the service of God, so we have found ourselves in Him and in all creation.

14.

Matters of Life and Death

Our life on earth is a preparation for the life beyond death when we approach more closely the understanding of eternity. But eternity is not simply an experience in store for us; it is in fact our constant dwelling place, even at this moment in time. We would know this if only we were fully aware of the glory that surrounds us. But the doors of our inner organs of perception are usually so firmly shut that we are impervious to all impressions except the coarsely material ones. This in itself is no bad thing, since our place of growth is where we find ourselves, and our tools of operation are the circumstances at hand. But if only we were aware, albeit dimly, of the destination ahead of us while we were about our earthly business, we could act more effectively and joyously. The beauty of this world would itself assume a renewed radiance. We would be less grasping and more compassionate, less demanding and more solicitous about the wants of other people. In this way, the apparently great divide between our earthly existence and the dimly perceived life beyond death would be narrowed and therefore more easily bridged.

There is, significantly, no incontrovertible evidence of survival of death, but as we grow more fully into our own identity so the continuation of life becomes increasingly certain to us. This identity, as we have already seen, is something more than all we hold dear and treasurable in ourselves; it embraces the identity of our neighbour also. It is then that our uniqueness, which is absolute, is shared so that it contributes to the whole of mankind, and we in turn receive the unique presence of those around us, so that in sharing and exchange we enter with increasing awareness the full Body of Christ. Ultimate reality is neither a fusion of the unit with the whole, nor a merging of the one with the many. It is, on the contrary, a union of the many into a whole that is all-embracing, whose centre and periphery is God.

It follows that in spiritual growth the establishment of full identity is also a growth into the knowledge of the love of God and the love of all our fellow beings, who become to us our most intimate neighbours. It is this vision of wholeness that should illumine the way of the counsellor, as he treads the path in the company of the many whom he ostensibly leads onward. In the spiritual life, the master is the servant of all, and his most characteristic action is that of washing the feet of his disciples. This washing of the foul-smelling feet of the lowly ones is, incidentally, not merely a gesture of humility and devotion; it also symbolises the preparatory work of the spiritual teacher in cleansing the surface of the psyche. When this is done, the Holy Spirit will be available – and welcome – to continue the cleansing, healing process at a deeper level.

When we begin to see every action and every relationship, every possession and every experience, as both the way towards eternal life and a sacrament of that life in the present moment, we are beginning to live in abundance. The counsellor, the one who channels and focuses the divine wisdom on to the psyche of his client, should know something of this full life and transmit that knowledge to those seeking help. This he does, as we have already seen, not so much by exhortation as by his transparency, not so much by description as by his radiance. In the end we do not describe what we have seen at the peak of the mountain of illumination; instead we enshrine it in our own personality and bring it down to earth with us. Just as to have seen Christ is to have seen the nature of the Father also, so to see the truly illumined person is to glimpse the glory and destiny of the human soul embodied perfectly in Christ.

Every relationship is a preparation for the consummation of love in eternal life. Therefore every relationship is sacred.

This does not mean that it must never be challenged, disturbed and even terminated, at least here on earth. But, as in the shattering encounter between Jacob and the angel of God, there must be no relinquishing of it until a blessing has been attained. The blessing is growth into a more mature person measured in terms of love and wisdom. As we grow in spiritual awareness so we come to see that those whom God has brought together – whether in marriage or in the looser ties of a professional collaboration or social relationship – can never be torn asunder. To be sure, the relationship seen in physical terms is by its very nature of limited duration. The vicissitudes of life and the irreversibility of death bring an end to all raptures of physical affection. But the soul is outside the physical order; it is our first private intimation of immortality. It was never meant to be alone or isolated. Indeed, as Heraclitus observed, one can never define the soul's boundaries, so deep are they.

The soul is the organ whereby we attain union with all that exists, and by the spirit within it we know God directly; His inner presence is attested by the Holy Spirit. A soul attachment goes on until the consummation of all things in God. When a relationship has been so destructive that a complete break has been essential for the survival of at least one of the parties concerned, the psychic link has to be cut – at least on the level of morbid attachment and subversive control.

The same is sometimes true of an extremely powerful personality, now deceased, who can still effect emotional pressure on the psyche of someone close to it who is still alive in the flesh. This is something more than an obsessive memory conditioning the life of the one who has suffered under that person; it is a direct presence that a psychically sensitive person can detect, often quite easily. The bad link has to be severed, but the one now freed from this psychic incubus – whether from a deceased or a living personality – has to start a new life of service and prayer, including prayer for his former tormentor. In the end we are all parts of the one body – the body of Christ, Who embraces all men irrespective of their religious belief – and we all have to be made whole according to the will of God.

Therefore, when a relationship has to be terminated on a mute note of failure here on earth – and this applies especially to a broken marriage – each party has to learn from the failure about his or her weaknesses and immature attitudes, so that during the remainder of earthly life there may be a more aware, less selfish approach to other people. In human relationships no dogmatic rule can be laid down because of the enormous variation that exists in the vast range of human personality and the complexity of the problems that so often arise. But one principle must not be overridden; the sanctity of each person irrespective of the evil of his actions. That which is perverse, anti-social and destructive in a person will require determined, unsentimental treatment that may extend far beyond the limits of this mortal life, but we are always called on to help rather than condemn. The ultimate means of help is prayer, especially when terrible retribution is striking at the foundation of an evil life. We can never relinquish another person even when absolute separation is mandatory on a physical level.

The end of all relationships is a closer union between man and God; that which is terminated in failure now will, we believe, also have its moment of reparation and triumph later in the life of the person in eternity. We have always to be open to this extended hope; admittedly it has a negative aspect of temporarily destructive, psychic influence that must be severed, but of greater ultimate importance is its positive, constructive promise of healing and redemption. The counsellor should be aware of these deeper springs of human relationships. He should neither work towards the continuance of every attachment, remembering that some are so deleterious that they ought to be terminated at once, nor should he ever fail to acknowledge that all attachments have their end in God, however remote it may appear in respect of their present aberration. Admittedly there lies an extended period of growth between what now prevails and the final divine realisation. Furthermore, this growth will be punctuated by suffering, renunciation, learning and service. In God nothing is lost. His face is that of the stranger whom the disciples met on the road to Emmaus. And it is the perpetual stranger on the way who, once accepted, leads us closer to God in Christ.

What I am saying is this: there are no bad experiences in life for the person who is open to the mystery of divine grace. When something that we regard as vital for our well-being has been summarily removed by the apparently impersonal inroads of fate, it will be replaced on a higher level of reality provided we have the faith to persist, to soldier on in the face of adversity. The end is to know ourselves and each other even as we are known by God and are, in eternal life, to know God also. One of the most valuable by-products of misfortune is its tendency to strip from the personality all social subterfuge. How important it is to be aware of the cesspit of anger, resentment and aggressiveness that lies deep in the psyche, but is so convincingly concealed by agreeable social attitudes in the run of daily life! But the personality will remain unformed until the darkness of hell within it is brought to the light of day and given its due respect also. Until it is acknowledged, accepted and loved – and this means allowed to express itself in full consciousness when we are secluded from our fellows – it can never be transmuted to forgiveness, compassion and service by the ever-available but all too infrequently sought grace of God.

There is a world of difference between the social theorist who speaks from the intellect of peace but whose life is an amalgam of ambition and crude manipulation of others and the saint who has no theories or ambitions any longer but who radiates peace from his humble presence. The theorist uses his ideas to protect himself from too wounding a self-knowledge. The saint knows himself so well that he needs no further protection: he also knows that all he possesses is in the hands of God, Who alone can transmute the dross of evil intentions into the gold of sacrificial love. 'If I climb up to heaven, thou art there; if I make my bed in Sheol, again I find thee' (Ps. 139:8). If we could only fathom the depths of God's love, we would know that He is with us in the darkness of hell no less than the radiance of celestial light; the passion of Christ reveals the first sequence and His resurrection and ascension the second.

The joy of counselling is to be able to guide the person in

difficulty on the road that leads to completion. This guidance is an aspect of companionship, not leadership. The techniques of psychotherapy can be of great value in releasing pent-up emotional material from the depths of the unconscious to the full light of awareness. But it is the assimilation of this material into the personality where it may form an integral part of our contribution to life that is the ultimate work. This is assisted by the enlightened counsellor under the guidance of the Holy Spirit. It is noteworthy that the most sceptical of the disciples, Thomas, was convinced of the reality of the risen Christ only when he saw the wounds of His passion. This is the authentic testimony of God's participation in the affairs of our world, that He was not merely a transcendent power or even an immanent principle of the soul, but that He took His place among us as a man among men and reached His ultimate veracity in His moment of greatest humiliation, when He visited us in the form of His Son. Likewise the testimony of a person's integrity is found in his creative response to suffering, so that it is incorporated into his personality and transformed into an instrument of compassion and service for his fellows. It should also be noted that suffering need not be on a grand scale. 'The heart knows its own bitterness, and a stranger has no part in its joy' (Prov. 14:10). It is when we have been demoted from our position of security or lowered from our point of vantage that we begin to participate psychically in the lives of other people; until then it is temptingly easy to play the Pharisee in Jesus' central parable, and thank God that we are so much better than our neighbour. The counsellor has to be stripped naked of all his illusions before he can be a reliable guide. Jesus says 'The gate that leads to life is small and the road is narrow, and those who find it are few' (Matt. 7:14). It is so under-populated because there are few who can bear to be freed of all inessential possessions.

Spiritual mastery is very different from the elitism inherent in most other provinces of human endeavour. It is constantly fascinating to behold the considerable range of spiritual understanding that is to be found in members of a single family. Of course, there is an equally inexplicable variation among individuals in the different skills of common life, such as athletic prowess, mathematical brilliance, artistic creativity or linguistic proficiency. It would seem that such individual skills are private matters, determining the life-style of the person for good or evil depending on how he uses them. In this respect, great physical beauty or intellectual brilliance can prove a stumbling-block to an unwary person by placing him on a pedestal of false esteem in the eyes of his peers, so that he feels superior to others. By contrast, our weaknesses cut us down to size so that we share fully in the lives of our most unfortunate neighbours. Indeed, God's power comes to its full strength in weakness, since His grace is all we need (2 Cor. 12:9). Spirituality, on the other hand, can never be sequestered in an individual, nor is anyone outside its influence. We are all called on to grow into a knowledge of God, in Whom alone the soul finds its rest and the person his fulfilment. Thus there is no isolated spiritual elite; the Master serves the beggar and gives His life for the sinner, so that all mankind may attain healing and be able to participate fully in the life of eternity. Those who reject God's love fail the test of life, but they proceed in labour and quest in the life beyond death; those who succeed will give of themselves more fully than before to their brethren who are in distress. The one closest to God is closest also to his neighbour – in eternal life no less than in the narrow confines of our social milieu.

Spirituality should also be distinguished from psychic sensitivity, while their close connection is acknowledged. That some people are more psychically attuned than others is a mystery of God's grace, but no more remarkable than outstanding ability in the fields of art or science. Such sensitivity is invaluable in effecting close relationships with other people, both here and in the life beyond death, but it can be used as easily to seduce and ensnare as to heal and liberate. Spiritual authority, on the other hand, is a product of experience.

Spirituality is acquired in the hard school of life when we

have, by slow and arduous progress, begun to assimilate the golden rule into our personalities: always treat others as you would like them to treat you; this is the Law and the prophets (Matt. 7:12). It is the vast range of spirituality that may be found in members of even a single family who share a common environment and a somewhat related heredity (though each person, apart from identical twins, is genetically unique) that leads one to consider the possibility of aspects of the personality, notably the soul, having enjoyed a previous existence.

However, there is no final solution to this fact of life. While heredity and environment no doubt play their part in fashioning the personality and determining the temperament, the inner core of spiritual excellence is of a different order. It is a special gift of the Holy Spirit to one who has travelled far on the road of renunciation, who has discovered the meretricious attractiveness and ephemeral duration of power and riches, beauty and fame. When all these illusions, these objects of vanity, dissolve into the mists of oblivion with the passage of time, the heart of love and wisdom stands firm, enduring the attrition wrought by suffering and ageing, and affording an inextinguishable beacon on the way to eternal life in God. Once the spiritual life is vibrant, the psychic sensitivity tends to become much more acute. It lies dormant in all of us, unlike intellectual or artistic mastery, which is the prerogative of the comparatively few. It is when we have attained spiritual insight that the psychic link becomes the means by which the Holy Spirit speaks from one soul to another, since in that state of coinherence (to repeat the term beloved by Charles Williams) we are indeed parts of the one body. This becomes no longer a mere theological assertion, but a fact of existence. In this respect psychic sensitivity divorced from spiritual understanding tends to separate one from one's fellows no less than do the other private gifts we have mentioned.

It seems paradoxical indeed that psychic sensitivity can have a divisive effect, since its function is to connect one person with another on a very deep level. However, one has only to witness the tendency to judge and disparage their neighbours that some psychically sensitive people exhibit, according to what they claim they can detect in them, to realise how separative and elitist that gift can be if it is not informed by the charity that comes with spiritual grace. Indeed, spiritual gifts alone bring us all together in love through the psychic empathy that follows prior union with God.

It is in fact another variation on the theme of the two great commandments: loving God first with one's whole being and then loving one's neighbour as oneself. The first must precede the second, but as the second grows in intensity, so the love of God becomes stronger. The spiritual gifts inform the psyche, and the psychic outpouring brings us closer to God.

Part of the work in any life is preparation for death. The period of retirement that should precede the final dissolution of all earthly ties provides an admirable means of entering the deepest knowledge of life. In the Hindu scheme of spiritual life, the aspirant proceeds from the stage of student to that of householder. This ends when his grandchildren are born. He then retires into the depths of the forest, alone or with his wife, where he proceeds to contemplate the deep things of existence. The last stage is one of complete renunciation, perhaps at a holy place, where he awaits death in a state of profound meditation. But it is important to understand that God, however He may be conceived, is the centre of all phases of this four-fold scheme of life: He is with the youth in his studies no less than in the arduous work of the householder or the contemplation of the mendicant. It is of interest that a not very dissimilar scheme of development attends the Jewish Kabbalist tradition, and that the deep secrets are withheld from those whose previous career has not rendered them worthy to receive them.

The almost completely secularly orientated Western man does not attend to matters so chilling in their immediacy as God and his own soul. These are swept aside in the hectic rush of daily acquisitive life. But the time comes when the old landmarks are swept away quite unceremoniously by the abrupt inroads of misfortune, illness and bereavement. All culminate in death, the moment of crisis and judgment. The counsellor for life is also a counsellor into death. Carl Jung has remarked in *The Soul and Death*, 'From the middle of life onward only he remains vitally alive who is ready to die with life'.

We begin to prepare for death when we cast an eye once more over past relationships, and see where reconciliation is possible in the light of truth. Grievances and points of radical disagreement cannot be summarily dismissed, let alone plastered over with insincere bonhomie. They should, however, be confronted, if possible, in mutual responsibility so that the conflicting parties can work together towards the resolution of the difficulty. For this way of reconciliation to succeed, there has to be a growing maturity in both parties. If one believes one has all the truth on one's side and cannot face the fact of one's own dark, shadow nature, one's intransigence (and that of the other person) will impede the way forward. In this case the matter has to be allowed to rest as quietly as possible, but we can proceed, at least in our own lives, in full awareness of the situation.

Prayer made ceaselessly to God not infrequently redeems a situation that seemed hopeless on a purely human level of reconciliation. The theme of confession and reconciliation is an autumnal approach to the ever-pressing advent of death. God alone forgives, and as we see the need for forgiving others, so we are brought closer to the footstool of the Almighty. 'If someone sues you, come to terms with him promptly while you are both on your way to court; otherwise he may hand you over to the judge, and the judge to the constable, and you will be put in jail. I tell you, once you are there you will not be let out till you have paid the last farthing' (Matt. 5:25–6). The right time to put our own house in order is always the present moment, and of no matter is this more pertinent than our bad relationships with other people. We can at least confess our sins to God and make what reparations are possible, without in any way trying to influence the other person in our favour by subtle emotional pressure.

The two great themes in working out a relationship are truth and reconciliation. The latter is very different from compromise; it means a growth in stature to accommodate another point of view by understanding and respecting the person who propounds it, which may be very different from one's own. Reconciliation pursued in honesty leads to the spiritual growth of all the parties concerned; its end is the gestation and birth of a new awareness of reality in which all the previously held views are seen to have been but the thoughts of little children. It is incidentally in this spirit alone that ecumenism in religion can succeed. The end is not to be a super-church that is able to smooth over and blur conflicting opinions, but a new church in God in which conflict is transmuted by illumined wisdom and healed by love. Indeed, we are told that in the new Jerusalem there is no Temple, for its temple is the sovereign Lord God and the Lamb (Rev. 21:22). In heaven our problems are solved by the Holy Spirit infusing our consciousness so that what was previously opaque to the understanding is now rendered transparent to the light of God. It is thus that the very commendable human desire for justice is fulfilled by the divine mercy and changed to universal love. We cease to care whether we get our just reward for our labour as we are about our Father's business in service to our brethren and healing of our neighbour. This is our privilege: to do the work of the One Who sent us. It is also the answer to the aggrieved labourers in the vineyard who were so shocked that those who started later on received the same wages as they who had begun the work early in the day (Matt. 20:1–16). In fact, the early labourers had the great advantage of being about God's work throughout the whole of their working life – seen figuratively as a day – whereas the latecomers enjoyed this happiness for only a comparatively short time. Nevertheless, the joy of coming to oneself, however late, cannot be measured in terms of material reward, hence the salary is the same for all.

Another important preparation for death that retirement brings is the work of disembarrassing oneself of possessions. Of course, our material possessions are bequeathed to those loved ones we leave behind after our death, but it is our secular power and reputation that are less comfortably relinquished. To learn to groom someone younger than oneself for the work ahead and then to move graciously but decisively out of the way, so as not to hamper him and his colleagues in the pursuit of new objectives, is a test of greatness of soul. As St John the Baptist said of his relationship with Jesus, 'As he grows greater, so I must grow less' (John 3:30). This is the meaning of love: to give of oneself without holding back anything for the well-being of another person. The way of Christ, who though rich became poor for us so that we through His poverty might become rich, is the way of the aspiring soul moving towards death. It is the supreme lesson of the spiritual life, and happy is the counsellor who can accompany the slowly dying person on this shadowy path full of glorious promise for those who tread on in faith and self-abandonment to the providence of God. As we grow in the spiritual life, so we prepare daily for our death by living ever more vibrantly in the moment. It is then that we cease to be entrapped in hard feelings, resentment and fear, and can flow out in love even to those who abuse us. When we are no longer there as an obstructive physical presence but are simply a representative of Him Who gave up His life for the world in the form of His only Son, we enter into eternal life now, and bring the promise of that life to all who meet us. Thus we move from the threat of death to the experience of immortality.

15.

Counselling for Death

To work alongside a person who is soon to make the transition we call death is one of the greatest privileges of spiritual counselling. Of course, on the purely factual level, no one knows exactly what lies beyond death – no traveller has returned with sufficient authenticity to provide us with the authoritative information. Even Jesus' appearances after the resurrection were distinctly fragmentary according to the tradition that has come down to us, and He left no account of what He had experienced during the period between His death and His resurrection. And yet, on an altogether deeper level, the soul spans the middle ground that includes both the present moment in time and the life of eternity. We begin to know the secret of survival as we come to a deeper knowledge of our own depths.

The privilege of acting as a companion, albeit discontinuously, to someone who is soon to die, is that one enters into the interim phase of life with him; as one encourages, so one is shown the light, and the advent of death loses its terror to become instead a welcoming light on the way to full development of the personality. A preoccupation with death is unhealthy inasmuch as it can easily degenerate into morbid curiosity and a way of evading the challenge of earthly existence. But when life on earth and death are seen as a continuous process, and the advent of death brings one more fully to life in the present moment, the preparation for death becomes the crowning glory of existence.

If death tells us anything at all it is this, that we should concentrate on the priorities of each passing moment, so that it may be spent as profitably and perfectly as possible.

This perfection mirrors the nature of God, and its essential quality is love. Therefore, when we begin to contemplate the great things of life, we are brought down to the one aspect that alone does not recede from us into a mist of insubstantiality. This is our relationship with other people, who, no doubt in a different form, will be there to meet us when we have been released from the body of our humiliation. Quoting St John of the Cross once more, when the evening comes we shall be judged on love.

The end of our life is a summary of the way we have treated our fellow men. It shows us how we have played our part in the greater world it has been our good fortune to encounter and experience. As we have sown, so we shall reap, except for the modifying factor of the forgiveness always available to the one who repents and opens himself to the inflow of divine love. Without forgiveness there is no love, without love no growth, without growth no continuing life. This pattern of soul development, I am persuaded, illuminates the life beyond death no less than our brief span on earth.

Death is a moment of recession and concentration. All our possessions recede from us, so that our domain, which may once have encompassed considerable estates and costly possessions, now finds its focus in a single room, ultimately a bed where we play out the final act of a life's drama. The three events which cancel the social and intellectual inequalities that play an apparently unfair part in our mortal life are misfortune, illness and death. *Misfortune* cuts the individual down to the size of a struggling child bereft of conceit and worldly wisdom. *Ill health* reduces him to a helpless child dependent on the goodwill of his friends and attendants. Though the rich man may have much more extensive quarters in which to live, his poor state of health precludes any real enjoyment of them; his last abode is to be a bed, perhaps at home or else in a hospital. The third inevitable event of life, which is *death*, is the absolute leveller of us all. The dying are freed from the incubus of their possessions, including the reputation they once boasted and the company they enjoyed. All they now have is the inner reality of the soul; what they have made of this during their stay on earth is the theme of their future concern in the new life ahead of them, and the basis of the judgment they will have to bear.

Few people confront the imminence of their death directly even when they know they are seriously ill. The spark of hope burns fiercely in the breasts of all who are psychologically balanced. It is right to affirm life rather than to deny it. The importance of life on earth is that it affords the personality an unsurpassed opportunity for growth into maturity. This maturing process, comparable to the bland warmth of an early autumn day, always involves relationships with our fellows on the hard terrain of practical, demanding physical encounter. Our earthly work is governed by the time-space environment in which we live. Time and space provide the disciplines under which we grow into self-regulating units. Time is an especially harsh taskmaster, urging us on and not permitting a delay in the right actions we are called on to perform. We work on a knife-edge of transience, but the fruit of the action of a moment may determine the quality of the remainder of our life on earth. Space limits the scope of our activity so that our effective work is restricted to a small area with a limited number of people.

It is salutary to consider the short time allowed to Jesus for His ministry – little more than three years – and the limited area in which He taught and served – merely that of Palestine. But every moment of His time with mankind was spent in intensive self-giving activity, the most important element of which was constant prayer. He died when He had completed His task, and among the more poignant of His utterances from the Cross were the words 'It is accomplished' (John 19:30). The full impact of His life, which had apparently ended on a mute note of failure, was in all probability hidden from Him at that stage as well as from those who considered themselves His disciples. Today the complex media of communication can transcend the limitations of space, bringing news and teaching to the remotest communities, but in the end it is the personal touch that matters; on this psychic communion depends the willingness of the newcomer to embrace the new teaching and carry it out in his daily life.

There is a time to die. This shows itself when one's worldly task has attained completion and one's personality is approaching integration. A premature death, especially one undergone in violent circumstances, can thwart this slow unfolding and maturation of the personality by curtailing the work in store for it. While God's final purpose cannot be frustrated, an interference in its fruition can impede the soul's growth and the person's service to the world. Therefore we should see that life is usefully prolonged, remembering that the soul grows in adversity no less than in prosperity. But a time comes when it is called to another realm, and then we should collaborate with nature in easing its onward passage. This does not imply what is called euthanasia. It is not our business to terminate life directly no matter how meaningless it may appear. But we can ease the person's onward passage to death by masterly inactivity. The practice of non-interference in another person's life is not to be confused with disinterest; it is, on the contrary, the deepest concern, which shows itself in loving action aimed at making the last part of life as tolerable as possible without attempting to prolong it artificially. The razor's edge between euthanasia on the one hand and a cruel prolongation of suffering on the other is traversed not so much by the guidance of human expertise as by the wisdom of the Holy Spirit given to those who pray assiduously. In other words, the dilemma is resolved not by legal sanction but by the inspiration of God. Furthermore each case is unique, a law unto itself.

When a person is facing death, he often knows intuitively that it is approaching, but tries to shield his loved ones from this knowledge. They in turn would most likely do their best to reassure him that he was going to recover, endeavouring to conceal their knowledge of the probable outcome from him. Should a person be told that he is shortly to die? My own experience suggests that an emphatic statement to that effect is seldom justified, even if the person asks directly. It is wiser to stress the seriousness of the condition, urging him to put his affairs in order if he has not already done so – and indeed our affairs should always be in order, for no one knows with certainty how any illness will terminate. The course of even such a fearful disease as widespread cancer is not as invariably relentless as some would think; while the great majority of cases deteriorate and die rapidly, a few may remain stationary for a considerable time and a very few may remit, or disappear, completely and permanently.

The more experience one has in the various disciplines of life, the less dogmatic does one become. Some people who are deeply religious and appear to believe in an afterlife are visibly shocked when the subject of their imminent death is broached in earnest; they seem to have little contact with their soul despite their religious beliefs. The same is not infrequently true of those who are interested in occultism and spiritualism; they may appear to be very knowledgeable about the fate of the discarnate soul in general, but are strangely remote from their own in particular. A person who is in contact with his own depths – and such an individual has a calm, silent repose about him – often knows the truth of his situation long before his medical attendants have come to a final conclusion, and he moves into the darkness of the unknown realm illumined by the light from within. Therefore it is wisest not to broach the subject of death until the dying person has done so, when it should be discussed openly and without fear. He should be made aware of the happiness in store for him as he moves effortlessly towards a new life. The process of dying is as gently progressive as is one's assisted movement on an escalator; one stands still in confidence as one is carried in the direction one seeks. It is the soul that is in charge, since the body is failing fast and the reasoning mind is completely out of its depth as a new, non-rational experience is upon it. A calm faith issues from the soul as the person is guided on the unknown, yet well-frequented, path to greater life – unknown to the personal consciousness yet well trodden in the collective unconscious. All this, of course, applies especially to the person who has lived a useful life in caring relationship with those around him.

In this respect the spiritual preparation for death is

something of a vastly different order from investigating matters psychical and 'occult'. These can, even if aspects of the teachings of various 'esoteric' schools are indeed accurate, serve to separate the person from his own centre and divert his attention from the living God into remote realms of speculation that have little to do with the urgent responsibilities of his present relationships with those around him. It is the deeper realities of the great mystical tradition of the world that should guide the thoughts of those who are moving towards the final point of earthly existence. The same realities should illumine the way of the counsellor in his great task of comfort and companionship for the dying.

As the soul breaks free from its physical moorings and lies more loosely in its relation to the body in which it worked faithfully for its own learning and for the resurrection of the body also, so it is able to effect psychic communion with the unseen world of eternity with a facility necessarily denied it during its time of densest incarnation. While we live creatively in the world, we function as a complete person with the properties of a person – body, mind, soul and spirit – acting in unity as a totality. Highly psychic people can be at a serious disadvantage if their working life is subject to constant disruption by the inflow of extraneous information of questionable practical use and great emotional tension. But when the time of bodily dissolution is at hand, the non-physical elements of the personality attain some degree of autonomy, so that they can function with an independence that would be impermissible during the time of active work in the world. It is not unusual for those close to death to get direct impressions of their friends and relatives now on the other side of life; the dying may be in direct communication with deceased colleagues. Numerous instances have been cited in which a dying person became apprised of the recent death of a friend through this type of communication; until then neither he nor members of his family had been aware of the demise of that person. The figure of a loved one may appear at the moment of death to take the person on his mysterious journey to the realms of the afterlife; sometimes this figure is a stranger, but its mission is the same. These apparitions are indeed hallucinations inasmuch as the object sensed has no physical reality and is a private experience. But their clarity and special relationship to the dying person together with the factual information they may impart suggest that they are not simply the product of a deranged mind.

All this is, of course, the preserve of psychical research, a subject that should be of at least some interest to anyone engaged in counselling, although some people respond more positively to its unusual manifestations than do others who may shun phenomena that lie outside the accepted canons of rational thinking. Be this as it may, the important point is that such phenomena, albeit of a private nature, should be treated with respect as possibly direct psychical communication between a dying person and members of his peer group who are now in the life beyond death. Our ignorance about these matters gives us no right to deride them or to dismiss them summarily as the psychopathology of a diseased brain. If we are open and humble we can learn much from what the dying are experiencing and attempting to tell us about the realms beyond death. This is part of the privilege of attending an alert, though dying, person.

As we are lifted beyond the mortal plane, so the vanities of our life are discarded, and we move in a realm of pure spirit where what we are as people comes across directly and without subterfuge. The same process of vigorous analysis confronts those who work with the dying; their insincerity and hypocrisy are mercilessly laid bare, as is the shallow learning of the person whose knowledge is acquired at second hand from books and lectures. Only those whose souls have been refined in the school of experience and whose wisdom has been gained in the vale of suffering can be useful counsellors to those on the way to a new life. In fact the same requirements are true of all counselling, but in the situation of death, their stark necessity is especially apparent. The counsellor should not impress on others his own views about survival of the personality so much as infuse a warm love and expectation by his presence. Likewise the use of Biblical texts is unhelpful until one can embody a text in one's own life. What is true to us flows from us to the person in need, because it comes from the heart and not merely the head. This statement should not be taken as a rejection of intellectual ways of attaining truth; it simply emphasises the need for private experience to confirm what we may believe on trust so as to make it credible to other people also. We give what we have experienced, and as we attend the final communications of those who are soon to die, so we are enlightened and comforted. The truth that all real communication is primarily psychic in quality is borne out by our relationship with dying friends no less than with those who seek our help because of an intractable personal problem. We do not supply the answer directly, but instead give the word that releases the power to think and act that was previously unavailable to the person in difficulty. It was unavailable because it was locked up in a psyche paralysed by fear and desolation.

The dying have to come to terms with their past life; those interesting cases of near-death experience in which a person has almost passed the point of no return from death but has been resuscitated just in time from a heart attack or an accident such as drowning or exposure to cold, tell of a panoramic playback of the past life of the individual with its salient features of crisis and choice. What the mind had stored over a period of many years is brought back to a completely changed consciousness in a matter of seconds. A similar raising of consciousness to cosmic proportions is a well-known concomitant of mystical experience. Sometimes the experience is one of blissful release that culminates in an encounter with a Christ-like figure of light who welcomes the newly-arrived person to a realm of fresh promise and understanding in the world of the life to come. Sometimes, however, the encounter may be quite horrifying. A great deal depends on the life the person had led before his precipitate encounter with death, from which he is bade to return to earthly life in order to finish work left behind. This work is in essence the perfection of his personality insofar as it may be achieved in the years of mortal life still granted to him.

Of course, a near-death experience is not exactly the same as the fate of the surviving aspects of the personality when death finally does occur. In a near-death experience the body is still in fact alive since the condition is reversible, whereas death, once it is established, is irreversible and final. Nevertheless, it is apparent that when a person hovers at an extremity of life, at the very point of transition to death, his spiritual state is what is claiming his complete attention. His moral balance-sheet is being surveyed, and its deficit may be of alarming magnitude. As we have noted previously, the prayer of a brave man making his spiritual journey to reality is that his unconscious may be made fully conscious, according to what he can bear. When we die this appears to happen whether or not we want it. Jesus tells us to use our worldly wealth to win friends for ourselves, so that when money is a thing of the past, we may be received into an eternal home. He also remarks that the worldly are more astute than the other-worldly in dealing with their own kind (Luke 16:8–9). This incidentally stresses the value of the things of this world in preparing us for the life beyond mortal death, when substance is consummated in spirit and our attitudes towards the sacredness of matter are now the measure of our spiritual stature in a realm where material objects cease to exist, but are now represented by a universal caring relationship. All mortal life is, in other words, a sacrament; every relationship is sacred, not only our human responsibilities but also our attitude to nature and inanimate objects. All have their place in God's creation, and anything that is ill-treated will bring its moment of retribution on the one who abused it. There is clearly a scale of values involved here; Jesus reminds us that we are worth more than the birds of the air, but nevertheless they also are part of God's providence, for He feeds them too (Matt. 6:26).

In near-death experiences that have followed suicide attempts, the person who has been rescued from premature death has been 'told' incontestably in the deepest level of his being that he had been breaking the rule of the game of life, and that there was indeed a purpose in continuing to live out his full span in this world. Our problems are indeed never removed by evading the fundamental issue of our own inadequacies; their solution requires the patient working-out of our difficulties in the light of honesty, faith and hard work. If we are foolish enough to believe that death brings to an end all our problems and cancels the just retribution in store for those who have acted wrongfully to their fellows, we shall soon be disabused of this misconception. The immediate state after death is as it is now except that we can no longer conceal our true disposition behind the beguiling mask of a dense physical body. Nor can we anchor our identity to our wealth, social position or intellectual eminence; all these belong to those whom we have left behind in this world. We have to go forward as naked as we were at the time of our birth with one great difference: we have now accompanying us a spiritual body composed of the thoughts, attitudes and desires brought with us from our span of life in this world. The finer our life has been, the more radiant is that spiritual body, and the more rapidly do we find ourselves greeted with affection by those whom once we knew in the flesh and who have preceded us in the life beyond death. They have come to welcome us to the place prepared for us by their solicitude, made possible by our own good actions, in the greater life beyond death. Jesus told His disciples, 'There are many dwelling-places in my Father's house; if it were not so I should have told you; for I am going there on purpose to prepare a place for you' (John 14:2). He goes on to promise that He will come again and receive them to Himself, so that where He is they may be also. This is the judgment: who will be there to receive us when we die? If our lives have been spent profitably in fostering love, we shall be received in love, and Christ will be available to us. If we have lived in spiritual squalor, abusing all those around us and separating ourselves from the springs of love in selfishness and gluttony, we shall be alone in darkness. This was the essential punishment that the man of wealth had to endure in the terrifying Parable of Lazarus and the Rich Man (Luke: 16:19–31).

It does not need the added embellishment of fire to make it a hellish experience; the isolation is punishment enough. And furthermore, there is a gulf between those who are in isolation and those in heavenly fellowship. It cannot be traversed simply by good intentions. Only a complete reappraisal of the misspent life can effect a release, as is seen in the far happier Parable of the Prodigal Son (Luke 15:11–32). I feel myself that these two teachings should be taken together, otherwise the punitive aspect of divine judgment would thwart the love which is God's intimate nature. Justice is always tempered by mercy provided the evil-doer confesses his sins and offers his renewed will as a surety for his future life of repentance and reparation. Love without justice interferes with the development of the human personality to spiritual proficiency, whereas justice without love would lead to the damnation of most of the human race. Fortunately in Christ we have One who has aligned Himself unequivocally with sinners, so that as soon as we confess our sins in His name, which is love, we are freed of an intolerable burden and can start to lead a new life in grace. That life will be hard, but its end is the redemption of all creatures from the law of death to the glory of eternal life in the company of the risen Christ.

With all this in the background, the one who is dying must be treated with great love. If he is a believer in God, the great metaphysical questions can be broached according to his physical and mental ability to participate in the discussion and his willingness to consider these matters at all. Some are eager to thrash out fundamental problems, while others are too ill or too apathetic to care very much about anything other than their immediate comfort. They should then be left in peace, while prayer goes on in the background of the counsellor's thoughts. This prayer is not so much for recovery as that the light of God's countenance may illuminate their darkness and shed its radiance on their perceptions during their final brief span on earth. Some dying people are acutely aware of the sinful, selfish life they used to lead; the kindness and tenderness shown to them by mere acquaintances may shame them into acknowledging the shallowness of their own previous emotional responses and the superficiality of their assessment of other people. 'Men judge by appearances but the Lord judges by the heart' (I Sam. 16:7). As the soul becomes more dominant in the failing body, so the moral sense becomes more acute in preparation by the greater judgment after death.

The counsellor can act as a very effective confessor provided he has a feeling for the ultimate questions of existence. The confessor does not judge; God alone can do this. His work is merely to give absolution and assure the penitent of God's forgiveness and unfailing love. When one speaks of God's love, one does not do it with the deliberation of a theologian. One pours it out to the person in need with that spontaneity that Jesus showed when He healed the sick, even in the austerity of the Temple on the Sabbath. To be able to pour out the love that is a presage of eternity on someone who is about to make the great transition that we call death is one of the counsellor's greatest joys. Death is then indeed swallowed up and victory won in the power of love, which alone can heal sin and bring the person into a proper relationship with God and his fellow creatures. To be sure, it is a priest's function to give formal absolution, but in the world of everyday life we may confess our sins to one another, and pray for one another. The end is healing, as we read at the conclusion of St James' letter (5:16). So much counselling work is in fact informal confession with the added dimension of understanding, so that the cause of the trouble can be healed as well as its effect. When a person has come to the end of his mortal life, the cause necessarily recedes into the background but the effects must be faced and redeemed by the power of love.

The same is true of the important work of bereavement counselling, now a discipline in its own right. Bereavement is a little death – an old way of life has gone and a stark period of loneliness confronts the one left behind. Loneliness with its usual corollary of living alone brings to the surface of consciousness the various repressed emotions of anger, resentment, guilt and especially fear. This fear is that of a gradually descending isolation, so that one may become as forgotten an entity as is, in one's darkest moments of desolation, the loved one on the other side of life. This is, in fact, another example of the crisis in identity that we have already considered. Just as the person made redundant lashes out in bitterness at his employers who have summarily discarded him on a scrap-heap of futility and waste, so the bereaved one rails at God, or fate, or his own bad luck – however he sees it in his own metaphysical scheme – while at the same time he regresses to the common childhood state of infuriated impotence from which few of us mature completely. When we cannot effect a change in our miserable condition, we make it our business to upset as many other people as possible so that they may be aware of our trouble and somehow come to our aid.

The mourning ritual is a most important psychological release reaction, and it should not be curbed. It is usually exacerbated during anniversaries and other private dates of significance. Only when the pent-up emotion is released and spent can a new life of apparent emptiness be faced. Then at last the Holy Spirit can enter into the space left behind by the loved one and all the emotions his death released. Hope springs in the shriven soul, and a new life can begin. The counsellor's work is to receive the impact of this emotional release, to bear its pain, and to be the instrument of hope whereby the Holy Spirit can bring a broader dimension of caring into the life of the bereaved one.

But there is also a communion between the living and the dead. The deceased person not infrequently makes his presence felt, sometimes by a sudden shaft of intense intellectual awareness, sometimes by a vision, an odour or even a voice. The most convincing and inspiring assurance that the beloved is still in spiritual communion with his loved one is a sudden consciousness of the love of God that lightens the darkness of bereavement and brings the sufferer to an inexpressible awareness that the deceased one is there but in a new form. He is surrounded by a radiance of an infinitely finer quality than anything he showed previously, even if he was a deeply spiritual person.

It is this experience of spiritual exaltation that tells us that all is well and that communion is now available on a truly spiritual level. The counsellor would be well advised to treat all such experiences with deep reverence, emphasising their factual message that the departed one is nearer his beloved than ever he was while still in the flesh. But experiences of this type are a gift from God; they are not to be sought – let alone cultivated. And their end is to bring the bereaved partner fully down to earth again, so that the last part of his own life may be especially productive in works of charity and service. Just as the risen Christ showed Himself most splendidly in the form of a stranger who walked and talked to His disciples on the road to Emmaus, so the spirit of the loved one comes to challenge his bereaved partner in the form of anyone who comes for succour and counsel. The work of the counsellor is to make this transition from devotion to a particular person, now deceased, to concern for many people constantly in proximity to the bereaved one, effective and complete. Before this happens, the psyche has to be laid bare and the nuances of psychic communion with the unseen experienced and analysed with intellectual astuteness as well as deep reverence.

If the hour that gives us mortal life is also preparing us for the time of death, then the experience of death in its many forms leads us to prepare more earnestly and devoutly for the life that does not end. This is the life of eternity in which we are one with God and united in each other.

16.

Intimations of Joy

The end of life, of which our short span on earth is but a presage of the eternal life to be known fully in the hereafter, is to be so united with the Lord and giver of life, the Holy Spirit, that one is in intimate fellowship with all that lives. This unencumbered communion with the creation in union with the Creator is the essence of joy. Joy is the soul's unending song as it goes about God's business in unselfconscious delight; this business is the healing and transmutation of all that is distorted and awry so that it may be re-formed in the divine image in which it was originally fashioned. When we work in effortless alignment with the cosmic flow, in unpremeditated collaboration with the divine will, with the exquisite precision of creative ecstasy, we know joy. Joy issues from the soul that is aware, free and creating new life under the guidance of the Holy Spirit.

Joy is of a different order of excellence from pleasure or even happiness. Both of these depend on the material state of well-being of the person and are related to the circumstances of his life; neither is permanent. It is hard to be happy when one is ill, in financial distress or surrounded by social turmoil or political upheaval. Pleasure is even more evanescent than happiness, depending as it does on an agreeable physical stimulus. Happiness may endure for a considerable period, but in the course of time its even flow and warm radiance are certain to be disrupted by bad tidings. Indeed, a state of undisturbed happiness, if it were to persist indefinitely, would impair the growth of the individual into a full person, someone of the stature of Christ himself. Job's happiness had to be completely swept away before he could come to a deeper understanding of his nature as a preparation for his great vision of God. The soul has to be stripped of all its vestments before its full stature can be revealed; these enveloping adornments are the favourable outer circumstances on which our happiness depends. The soul has to be rendered naked of all possessions, to have nothing but its own being, before it can know the presence of God in that intimate relationship which is the source of all love and wisdom. This was the final requirement that Jesus demanded of the rich young man who had fulfilled the commandments of the Law but still clung for security to his wealth. Anything that shields the soul from its ultimate encounter with the living God is an incubus which has to be shed. Happiness can therefore act paradoxically against our knowing ourselves fully and being open to the self-revealing love of God.

Should we therefore not seek happiness for ourselves and for others? Assuredly, but only after the greater gift has been attained: a knowledge of the love of God. In the words of Christ, 'Set your mind on God's kingdom and His justice before everything else, and all the rest will come to you as well' (Matt. 6:33). It is an unfortunate fact of life that most of us cultivate a state of self-absorbed comfort; this often has to be shattered by a disaster before we are impelled to start the great journey of the mind to God's kingdom and His justice.

The soul that is naked of all encumbrances, including those that would serve to adorn it, can lay itself open to the pervading radiance of the Holy Spirit in trust and self-giving love. In the story of the Creation our two primaeval ancestors Adam and Eve are both naked, the man and his wife, and they have no feeling of shame towards one another (Genesis 2:25). As soon as they grasp after individual power that comes from a human knowledge of good and evil separate from the love of God, which alone raises knowledge to the stature of wisdom, they find their nakedness a cause for shame. In other words, sex is deprived of its primal quality as a gift of intimate, self-giving relationship between one person and another. Instead it becomes degraded and contaminated with lust, so that one person uses it to dominate another for his own pleasure. The I-Thou relationship with God as its centre becomes an I-It relationship with human desire at the centre. Once the soul is disembarrassed of all desire except to do the will of God Whose presence is known in its centre, or spirit, it returns to its radiant nakedness, and its beautiful song can once more peal forth in sounds of exultation as it was at the beginning.

This return to innocence is of a different order from the pristine innocence of childhood; it is a purity of perception informed by compassion, fertilised by love and crowned by wisdom. In other words, the various misfortunes that brand any human life are not simply to be dismissed as the fruit of error, as events that need not have occurred if only the person had been less foolish and more obedient to the law of life. They are, on the contrary, to be seen as the way of purification, the means of sanctification. The mission of Christ was to set fire to the earth. He had a baptism of death to undergo, and great was the restraint He was under until the ordeal was over. Far from establishing peace on earth, He had come to bring division (Luke 12:49–53). Until every aspect of the personality is revealed and brought to the light of full consciousness, it will emit a confusing miasma that will obstruct the person from fulfilling his destiny, from doing the work God has set before him. That which acts with evil intent has first to be unmasked and revealed; then it is to be accepted and understood. Its intent can be changed to good only when it is loved and given to God in prayer. The good that such an incubus, now healed, can provide is a compassionate understanding of other people's defects and a growing concern for all life. This shows itself practically in being more effective in our service and more open in our love for all beings than we were in the days of our spiritual blindness, when we believed that our character was clear of all frailty and that the peace we knew was of God when, in fact, it was simply a smug complacency. No one in the company of Jesus could continue to harbour such an illusion. Likewise, the naked soul of a truly holy person acts as an unclouded mirror in which those who come to him for spiritual guidance can see themselves clearly and devastatingly, and yet with acceptance and forgiveness.

The naked soul sings its paeans of joy as it knows the Holy Spirit directly and can respond with rapt attention and total dedication. It has lost all selfish concern in the light of a truth so absolute that it is illuminated by the Spirit of God that dwells in its own spirit. It is indeed one in spirit with God. This unity is no longer merely a theological affirmation; it is a fact of existence proved by the transformation of the personality effected by the Holy Spirit. As the soul reflects as in a mirror the splendour of the Lord, so it is transfigured into His likeness from splendour to splendour. This is the influence of the Lord who is spirit (2 Cor. 3:18). The moment of joy is precipitated by a direct vision of the divine. To be sure, the totality of God is beyond the compass of the human mind, but even the least of us is privileged to have shafts of unimpeded spiritual awareness in which the divine energies impinge themselves directly on the soul. In other words, God, though transcendent of all categories of human thought and described more fittingly in negative terms than in words of discursive intelligence, comes to the naked soul in a personal form of caring and blessing. He lifts up our faltering hearts to the peaks of aspiration; He infuses our spirit with the glory of His effulgent radiance, so that we know Him as we are raised up to His benediction.

The vision of God's presence is preceded by an inner cleansing of the portals through which we perceive truth whether in its intellectual mode, its aesthetic utterance or its altruistic thrust. To speak of truth in categories other than the intellectual would seem to be an unnecessary extension of this word. But in God, as made manifest in Christ, the way, the truth and the life are one. All that leads us to a quickened perception or heightened awareness of divine reality is of the nature of truth. This may be a scientific discovery or a philosophical understanding that suddenly illuminates the mystery of material existence in a new way. It may be a masterpiece of art that reveals in aesthetic intensity through the logic of form the exquisite radiance of the world around us and the mind of God that unceasingly fashions

that world. It may be a moment of self-giving love which
tears away the citadel of the ego, thereby removing all that is
obstructive and predatory in the personality, rendering the
soul in its inmost recesses naked in innocent openness to
God.

Whenever the inhibitions of fear – a fear based on
insecurity and self-distrust – are torn away, the soul is freed
to express its true nature, which is joy, in the light of the
Holy Spirit that illuminates it from within its centre as well
as from beyond all tangible, intelligible limits. The soul's
limits are indefinable in their depth and extent, but in
personal consciousness we tend, by our egoistical preoccupation with the world around us, to contract into a hard
ball of uncommunicative matter. This apparent contraction
of the soul serves to limit the extent of its participation in
life, and to occlude the light of God from impinging fully on
us. In this way the soul is immured in the dross of personal
desire. It lies concealed behind rubbish, and prevented from
attaining full psychic communion with our fellow creatures.
As a result it becomes shrunken, opaque and desiccated, as
the blood and water of life are squeezed out of it, and it
contracts into an inert shell.

But when the light of God breaks through into our feeble
consciousness once more, the soul revives, breathes in the
power of the Holy Spirit, and responds to the world's call for
help and love. Then we live again. As St John puts it, 'We for
our part have crossed over from death to life: this we know
because we love our brothers' (1 John 3:14).

This is our first glimpse of resurrection, when the
consciousness of inner concern moves from its customary
focus within us to extend towards the periphery of life, in
order to embrace someone outside us. This moment of new
life articulated by the soul is what we experience as joy. It is
not dependent on what we are receiving – as are pleasure and
happiness – but on what we are giving. The source of joy is
witnessing the beloved – who is potentially everyone –
growing into a deeper knowledge of God's love, as it is
transformed radiantly in the love of God. To see
understanding enter a child's mind as it is taught its first

lessons, to witness the subtle interplay of recognition as it plays over the face of an alienated person who was, until then, separated from all outer concerns, to watch sight return to the blind and those without hope renewing their trust in mankind following the devoted service they have received – all this is a source of joy. Joy is shared between the one who receives the gift and the one who witnesses its advent in the life of the other. It is mutual and spontaneous. It is a sudden recognition that God's providence illumines all things and directs all events, so that they are rendered new and full of meaning, that each points a way of direct access to the advent of full participation in the divine nature.

It is the privilege of those concerned in the counselling process to lead the client to the joy of recognition that all is well for those who put their trust in the creative potentiality of life, who are open to God's self-revealing providence. The counsellor's soul should radiate that joy; he should be so far outside himself and the limitations of his own understanding that his vision can glimpse the glory beyond rational definition. In that state he can communicate directly with the soul of the one who comes for help. Joy kindles the fearful personality with trust that issues forth in fruitful endeavour, so that its soul blazes triumphantly in a new work enlightened by the spirit within. To be sure, this noble intent of starting a new life has to be implemented by a renewed, strengthened will, deep understanding and acceptance of what has occurred, and the humility to learn from previous experiences as well as from the insights of other people, even those whom one might previously have dismissed summarily as being of little account. Joy is contained in a rare glimpse into the ultimate future, which is also the eternal present, that all is well and that the path of life has a direction, a destination and an end. It is the inspired answer to the contrary proposition, often only too plausible after a disheartening day's work that 'life is a tale told by an idiot, full of sound and fury, signifying nothing'. The refutation of this view is not philosophical. It is afforded by the soul's vision, articulated in hope and consummated in loving service to the world.

Joy is the second fruit of the spirit (Gal. 5:22). It follows love, which is God's revelation of Himself to us; together they bring peace. This is an absence of personal striving for rewards and recognition, so that one can be wholeheartedly about God's business in perfect alignment to His will, bringing love and joy to all who are open and willing to receive them. When we are so centred and grounded in our own being that we can accept ourselves as we are and then forget ourselves, we can entrust ourselves to God's will and start to do what He has prepared for us. This is joy, to be eternally about God's business which brings release from bondage to the ego and freedom to be oneself in the image of Christ. Therein lies healing: this is the end of the work of counselling. We remember the words of Dame Julian of Norwich, 'He did not say, "Thou shalt not be tempested, thou shalt not be travailed, thou shalt not be afflicted", but He said, "Thou shalt not be overcome". He willed that we take heed of these words, and that we be ever strong in sure trust, in weal and woe. For He loveth and enjoyeth us, and so willeth He that we love and enjoy Him and mightily trust in Him; and all shall be well' (*Revelations of Divine Love*, chap. 68). Those are the words of joy that issue forth from the centre of the soul of the counsellor. How different in tone and import they are from the glib assurances that are uttered by the unfeeling tongue! The personality behind such encouragement is like a dead body.

Joy prevails even when circumstances are threatening and failure seems certain to crown all our efforts. Even if this world were to go up in smoke, joy would not end. For God creates new heavens and a new earth so that the past will not be remembered and will come no more to men's minds (Isa. 65:17). In the new dispensation there will no longer be any sea (Rev. 21:1). The sea symbolises evil; it is also the symbol of the unconscious with its multitudinous repressed complexes and their potent emotional charge. In the new Jerusalem there is no need for organised religion, no temple cultus, since the Lord God and the Lamb are the temple (Rev. 21:22). The unconscious is now fully conscious and its destructive elements are redeemed and transfigured by God

Who is no longer concealed in the spirit of the soul, but radiates from the substance of the personality and brings light to all those in its proximity. In the new Jerusalem, which itself is a symbol both of redeemed humanity and the enlightened human soul, the city does not need the sun or moon for light, since it is illuminated by God's radiant glory, and the Lamb acts as a lamp (Rev. 21:23). That light serves to fulfil Jeremiah's earlier central prophecy about the new covenant God will make with Israel: He will set His Law within them, writing it on their hearts. Then He shall become their God and they His people (Jer. 31:33–4). Religious instruction shall fade away before the presence of God immanent in the soul, Who is the source of all understanding, the fountain of all wisdom, the seat of all counsel. He is the life that is the light of men, a light that shines on in the darkness which has never mastered it (John 1:4–5).

To know that light is mystical illumination, to bring it down to the world of matter is joy, to be its agent in service to that world is freedom and peace. The end of the counselling process is to set before each person the truth of his own being, that God lies within him, and that he needs no help outside God to bring him to the freedom of a fully actualised person. The traditional psychotherapeutic process with its analytic overtones can reveal and clarify much unconscious material, sorting out the debris and organising the psychic life into a coherent pattern. Orderliness is a primary function of the Holy Spirit.

But then comes the work of transmutation, in which the therapist or counsellor takes on the burden of the psychic disorder of the client, and is the agent of substitution, exchange, healing and restoration. The problem is not so much disposed of as transfigured in the light of counsel and love to a radiance of universal health. It now becomes a sign of healing for many who are oppressed with their own burden. This transfiguration is effected in the place of the soul where the inner light of the spirit burns. The joy radiating from the place of light accompanies the power and love that potentiate the healing process. The transfiguration is instantaneous in its action, but its effects show themselves only by degrees in the life of the person rising from affliction to health.

Few of us could bear a sudden, complete psychic healing. The burden of absolute health would be intolerable in the responsibility it brought with it; the change in life-style would be too dramatic to accommodate all at once. Furthermore, the healing power of the Holy Spirit has to quicken the entire frame of the physical body no less than every perverse thought and destructive emotion that is released by the unredeemed, ailing psyche. As health emerges unobtrusively from the depths of the purged personality, so does joy hesitantly radiate from the open soul, now cleared of egoistical barriers and cleansed of the effect of adverse conditioning. The emergence of joy is like the slow advent of the rising sun on a distant horizon: it starts as a delicate, suffused glow that seems gradually to gain the courage of momentum until its light fully heralds the dawn of a new day. This joy is a confirmation of faith made real by God's mighty healing act and fully established in a life of health. Joy is the end of the healing process, but it also initiates healing under the direction of the Holy Spirit.

Joy grows under adversity inasmuch as suffering strips the soul naked of all outer accretions. Joy grows in intensity through the work of counselling and healing other people: the more we give of ourself in selfless service, the more we receive of the Holy Spirit. Eventually we become an immaculate instrument for the work of the Holy Spirit – as we get ourself out of the way, so the personality is transformed and our very presence becomes a focus of blessing to all in our vicinity. The joy of this enlightened presence kindles joy in the depths of all who come into proximity with us; their difficulties seem to fall into place and can be dealt with positively, while at the same time the natural healing power of the body, now freed of emotional strain, can correct the minor disabilities that life in the world brings with it.

Joy therefore cannot be cultivated. It is evoked as we attain the freedom necessary to establish our true identity, that of a child of God, made in the image of Jesus Christ. The more we grow into what we are to be, the more all our disabilities fall into place in the scheme of our life's unfolding, and each contributes, in its healed aspect, to our full life in God. When we are nothing, we are everything, for then we know Him as the supreme No-Thing from Whom all that exists finds its creative source. He is known to us as love, which is exquisitely personal in its concern, and we respond with the soul's song of joy. The end is peace, to do God's will in harmony with each other in His presence. The soul that has found its rest in God, to return once more to St Augustine's thought, is at peace with God, with its fellows and with itself. It does as it wills since it is moved by love. And that love brings all sentient beings into fellowship with each other in God. The cosmic music of joy is the eternal celebration of this love and peace, this goodwill among men, and the resurrection of all things to full spirit.

The End of Counsel

The counsellor is the instrument of the Holy Spirit. His work is to impart the wisdom of God in words of gentle understanding to the perplexed, the harassed and the fearful. Those who are perplexed see the light of God's purpose in their lives, the harassed are given the balm of God's peace, and the fearful are filled with the radiance of God's love.

When the growing knowledge that emerges from painstaking scientific research into the mainsprings of human behaviour is illuminated by the wisdom of God that pours from the counsellor in the self-abandon of deep silence, a deeper, more comprehensive understanding is born that can lighten the darkness of the person in emotional turmoil and bring rest to the distraught soul. The answer is an intimately private one between God and the soul of the person who seeks in diligence and faith. The counsellor aids in transmitting the message through his psychic rapport with the client and his open availability to the Holy Spirit. The spirit of counsel imparts power as well as understanding, spiritual authority as well as guidance.

It was prophesied by a follower in the tradition of Isaiah,

The spirit of the Lord God is upon me because the Lord has anointed me; he has sent me to bring good news to the humble, to bind up the broken-hearted, to proclaim liberty to captives and release to those in prison; to proclaim a year of the Lord's favour and a day of the vengeance of our God; to comfort all who mourn, to give them garlands instead of ashes, oil of gladness instead of mourners' tears, a garment of splendour for the heavy heart (Isa. 61:1-3).

This is the end of counsel: to bring light to those who have lived in the darkness of self-denigration, to set free those who are bound in chains of destructive emotions and negative thoughts. The unobstructed availability and constant devotion of the counsellor to both God and man enables him to transmit the divine message to those in need with stern authority no less than in tender compassion. But the end is hope, not denunciation.

The summation is to bring as many people as possible to the freedom that comes with self-knowledge and to the stability of an identity that has its roots in truth. To be anchored in the security of God's love will alone prevent one's sense of identity fluctuating precariously according to the circumstances that play around one. The truth that sets us free is our universal quest; it directs the counsellor on the path towards proficiency, and is his priceless gift to all those who seek his assistance so that they too can be free and of service to others. As one traverses the hard terrain of mortal life disfigured with its manifold hazards and pitfalls, so one slowly becomes a manifold guide to those on the road of self-actualisation, to the end that they may become real, independent people. It is a great privilege to be able to show the way towards freedom, to help someone become more authentically himself. This is the inspiring work of all who are called upon to enter the ministry of counselling.